BILLY THE KID
The Best Writings on the Infamous Outlaw

HAROLD DELLINGER

TWODOT®

GUILFORD, CONNECTICUT
HELENA, MONTANA
AN IMPRINT OF THE GLOBE PEQUOT PRESS

A · T W O D O T® · B O O K

Text design by Sheryl Kober

Library of Congress Cataloging-in-Publication Data
Billy the Kid : the best writings on the infamous outlaw /
[compiled by] Harold Dellinger.
    p. cm.
 Filmography: p.
 ISBN 978-0-7627-4893-8
 1. Billy, the Kid. 2. Outlaws—Southwest, New—Biography.
3. Southwest, New—Biography. 4. Billy, the Kid—In literature.
5. Outlaws—Southwest, New—Historiography. 6. Southwest,
New—Historiography. I. Dellinger, Harold.
 F786.B54B5 2008
 364.15'52092—dc22
 [B]
                                    2008031260

Printed in the United States of America
10 9 8 7 6 5 4 3 2 1

CONTENTS

———◦•◦———

FOREWORD

———◆·◆·◆———

"Resist much, obey little."
—WALT WHITMAN

In many ways, Henry McCarty (aka, Billy the Kid, Kid Antrim, and William H. Bonney) is a difficult guy to get to know. For every fact that is generally accepted, there are a dozen that continue to be debated.

A product of a difficult time and a bloody place, his legacy has come to be an unlikely mix of rumor, fact, and outright myth. A young man when he died, probably only twenty-one, he's been accused of committing as many as the same number of homicides (the reality is probably much lower). His reputation was built on New Mexico's Lincoln County War, a conflict in which he was seen as both hero and victim. Buck-toothed and blue-eyed, the only indisputed, surviving photo of him shows a boy staring dumbly at the camera; yet his letters to the Governor of New Mexico show him to be quite literate. An icon of the West, he was likely born in Manhattan. The contradictions and ironies go on and on.

In compiling these pieces, I've tried to show the Kid from a number of different perspectives. From the earliest authors (some writing with a delightful energy and enthusiasm), to the later, more authoritative pieces, from dime novelists to poets, Billy the Kid has been a blank canvas, a figure on which authors have been able to project their own thoughts and feeling, bolstering the mythology even while creating an impressive body of art.

I have made selections from a herd of very good books on Billy the Kid. Whether you're a first-time reader or a longtime afficionado, I do hope you find something here to enjoy.

GUNSLINGER, BOOK I

By Edward Dorn

—◆◆◆—

The curtain might rise
Anywhere on a single speaker

I met in Mesilla
The Cautious Gunslinger
of impeccable personal smoothness
and slender leather encased hands
folded casually
to make his knock.
He would show you his map.
There is your domain.
Is it the domicile it looks to be
or simply a retinal block
of seats in,
he will flip the phrase
the theater of impatience.

    If it is where you are,
the footstep in the flat above
in a foreign land
or any shimmer the city
sends you

the prompt sounds
of a metropolitan nearness
     he will unroll the map of locations.
His knock resounds
inside its own smile, where?
I ask him is my heart.
Not this pump he answers
artificial already and bound
touching me
with his leathern finger
as the Queen of Hearts burns
from his gauntlet into my eyes.
     Flageolets of fire
he says there will be.
This is for your sadly missing heart
the girl you left
in Juarez, the blank
political days press her now
in the narrow adobe
confines of the river town
her dress is torn
by the misadventure of
     her gothic search
The mission bells are ringing
in Kansas.
Have you left something out:
Negative, says my Gunslinger,
no *thing* is omitted.

EMERSON HOUGH
THE STORY OF THE OUTLAW

This early study of the Western desperado and how he got to be that way is a representative view of how Billy the Kid was viewed at the turn of the twentieth century. What Hough calls "historical" and "scientific" studies clearly place Billy the Kid in the Western desperado category.

The prolific Hough grew up on the frontier and used the experience to fashion a long writing career. His historical novels The Mississippi Bubble *(1902) and* The Covered Wagon *(1922) were among his other big hits in a career that stretched from the 1880s to the 1920s.*

EXCERPT FROM

THE STORY OF THE OUTLAW

A Study of the Western Desperado

With historical narratives of famous outlaws; the stories of noted border wars; vigilante movements and armed conflicts on the border.

By Emerson Hough

1905

———————

Who and what was the bad man? Scientifically and historically he was even as you and I. Whence did he come? From any and all places. What did he look like? He came in all sorts and shapes, all colors and sizes—just as cowards do. As to knowing him, the only way was by trying him. His reputation, true or false, just or unjust, became, of course, the herald of the bad man in due time. The "killer" of a Western town might be known throughout the state or in several states. His reputation might long outlast that of able statesmen and public benefactors.

What distinguished the bad man in peculiarity from his fellowman? Why was he better with weapons? What is courage, in the last analysis? We ought to be able to answer these questions in a purely scientific way. We have machines for photographing relative quickness of thought and muscular action. We are able to record the varying speeds of impulse transmission in the nerves of different individuals. If you were picking out a bad man, would you select one who, on the machine, showed a dilatory nerve response? Hardly. The relative fitness for a man to be "bad," to become extraordinarily quick and skillful with weapons, could, without doubt, be predetermined largely by these scientific measurements. Of course, having no thought-machines in the early West, they got at the matter by experimenting, and so, very often, by a graveyard route. You could not always stop to feel the pulse of a suspected killer.

The use of firearms with swiftness and accuracy was necessary in the calling of the desperado, after fate had marked him and set him apart for the inevitable, though possibly long-deferred, end. This skill with weapons was a natural gift in the case of nearly every man who attained great reputation whether as killer of victims or as killer of killers. Practice assisted in proficiency, but a Wild Bill or a Slade or a Billy the Kid was born and not made.

Quickness in nerve action is usually backed with good digestion, and hard life in the open is good medicine for the latter. This, however, does not wholly cover the case. A slow man also might be a brave man. Sooner or later, if he went into the desperado business on either side of the game, he would fall before the man who was brave as himself and a fraction faster with the gun.

There were unknown numbers of potential bad men who died mute and inglorious after a life spent at a desk or a plow. They might have been bad if matters had shaped right for that. Each war brings out its own heroes from unsuspected places; each sudden emergency summons its own fit man. Say that a man took to the use of weapons, and found himself arbiter of life and death with lesser animals, and able to grant them either at a distance. He went on, pleased with his growing skill with firearms. He discovered that as the sword had in one age of the world lengthened the human arm, so did the six-shooter—that epochal instrument, invented at precisely that time of the American life when the human arm needed lengthening—extend and strengthen his arm, and make him and all men equal. The user of weapons felt his powers increased. So now, in time, there came to him a moment of danger. There was his enemy. There was the affront, the challenge. Perhaps it was male against male, a matter of sex, prolific always in bloodshed. It might be a matter of property, or perhaps it was some taunt as to his own personal courage. Perhaps alcohol came into the question, as was often the case. For one reason or the other, it came to the ordeal of combat. It was the undelegated right of one individual against that of another. The law was not invoked—the law would not serve. Even as the quicker set of nerves flashed into action, the arm shot forward, and there smote the point of flame as did once the point of steel. The victim fell, his own weapon clutched in his hand, a fraction too late. The law cleared the killer. It was "self-defense." "It was an even break," his fellowmen said; although thereafter they were more reticent with him and sought him out less frequently.

"It was an even break," said the killer to himself—"an even break, him or me." But, perhaps, the repetition of this did not serve to blot out a certain mental picture. I have had a bad man tell me that he killed his second man to get rid of the mental image of his first victim.

But this exigency might arise again; indeed, most frequently did arise. Again the embryo bad man was the quicker. His self-approbation now, perhaps, began to grow. This was the crucial time of his life. He might go on now and become a bad man, or he might cheapen and become an imitation desperado. In either event, his third man left him still more confident. His courage and his skill in weapons gave him assuredness and ease at the time of an encounter. He was now becoming a specialist. Time did the rest, until at length they buried him.

The bad man of genuine sort rarely looked the part assigned to him in the popular imagination. The long-haired blusterer, adorned with a dialect that never was spoken, serves very well in fiction about the West, but that is not the real thing. The most dangerous man was apt to be quiet and smooth-spoken. When an antagonist blustered and threatened, the most dangerous man only felt rising in his own soul, keen and stern, that strange exultation which often comes with combat for the man naturally brave. A Western officer of established reputation once said to me, while speaking of a recent personal difficulty into which he had been forced: "I hadn't been in anything of that sort for years, and I wished I was out of it. Then I said to myself, 'Is it true that you are getting old—have you lost your nerve?' Then all at once the old feeling came over me, and I was just like I used to be. I felt calm and happy, and I laughed after that. I jerked my gun and shoved it into his stomach. He put up his hands and apologized. 'I will give you a hundred dollars now,' he said, 'if you will tell me where you got that gun.' I suppose I was a trifle quick for him."

The virtue of the "drop" was eminently respected among bad men. Sometimes, however, men were killed in the last desperate conviction that no man on earth was as quick as they. What came near being an incident of that kind was related by a noted Western sheriff.

"Down on the edge of the Pecos valley," said he, "a dozen miles below old Fort Sumner, there used to be a little saloon, and I once captured a man there. He came in from somewhere east of our territory, and was wanted for murder. The reward offered for him was twelve hundred dollars. Since he was a stranger, none of us knew him, but the sheriff's descriptions sent in said he had a freckled face, small hands, and a red spot in one eye. I heard that there was a new saloon-keeper in there, and thought he might be the man, so I took a deputy and went down one day to see about it.

"I told my deputy not to shoot until he saw me go after my gun. I didn't want to hold the man up unless he was the right one, and I wanted to be sure about that identification mark in the eye. Now, when a bartender is waiting on you, he will never look you in the face until just as you raise your glass to drink. I told my deputy that we would order a couple of drinks, and so get a chance to look this fellow in the eye. When he looked up, I did look him in the eye, and there was the red spot!

"I dropped my glass and jerked my gun and covered him, but he just wouldn't put up his hands for a while. I didn't want to kill him, but I thought I surely would have to. He kept both of his hands resting on the bar, and I knew he had a gun within three feet of him somewhere. At last slowly he gave in. I treated him well, as I always did a prisoner, told him we would square it if we had made any mistake. We put irons on him and started for Las Vegas with him in a wagon. The next morning, out on the trail, he confessed everything to me. We turned him over, and later he was tried and hung. I always considered him to be a pretty bad man. So far as the result was concerned, he might about as well have gone after his gun. I certainly thought that was what he was going to do. He had sand. I could just see him stand there and balance the chances in his mind."

"Another of the nerviest men I ever ran up against," the same officer went on, reflectively, "I met when I was sheriff of Dona Aña county, New Mexico. I was in Las Cruces, when there came in a sheriff from over in the Indian Nations looking for a fugitive who had broken out of a penitentiary after killing a guard and another man or so. This sheriff told me that the criminal in question was the most desperate man he had ever known, and that no matter how we came on him, he would put up a fight and we would have to kill him before we could take him. We located our man, who was cooking on a ranch six or eight miles out of town. I told the sheriff to stay in town, because the man would know him and would not know us. I had a Mexican deputy along with me.

"I put out my deputy on one side of the house and went in. I found my man just wiping his hands on a towel after washing his dishes. I threw down on him, and he answered by smashing me in the face, and then jumping through the window like a squirrel. I caught at him and tore the shirt off his back, but I didn't stop him. Then I ran out of the door and caught him on the porch. I did not want to kill him, so I struck him over the head with the handcuffs I had ready for him. He dropped, but came up like a flash, and struck me so hard with his fist that I was badly jarred. We fought hammer and tongs for a while, but at length he broke away, sprang through the door, and ran down the hall. He was going to his room after his gun. At that moment my Mexican came in, and having no sentiment about it, just whaled away and shot him in the back, killing him on the spot. The doctors said when they examined this man's body that he was the most perfect physical specimen they had ever seen. I can testify that he was a fighter. The sheriff offered me the reward, but I wouldn't take any of it. I told him that I would be over in his country some time, and that I was sure he would do as much for me if I needed his help. I hope that if I do have to go after his particular sort of bad people, I'll be lucky in getting the first start on my man. That man was as desperate a fighter as I ever saw or expect to see. Give a man of that stripe any kind of a show and he's going to kill you, that's all. He knows that he has no chance under the law.

"Sometimes they got away with desperate chances, too, as many a peace officer has learned to his cost. The only way to go after such a man is to go prepared, and then to give him no earthly show to get the best of you. I don't mean that an officer ought to shoot down a man if he has a show to take his prisoner alive; but I do mean that he ought to remember that he may be pitted against a man who is just as brave as he is, and just as good with a gun, and who is fighting for his life."

Of course, such a man as this, whether confronted by an officer of the law or by another man against whom he has a personal grudge, or who has in any way challenged him to the ordeal of weapons, was steadfast in his own belief that he was as brave as any, and as quick with weapons. Thus, until at length he met his master in the law of human progress and civilization, he simply added to his own list of victims, or was added to the list of another of his own sort. For a very long time, moreover, there existed a great region on the frontier where the law could not protect. There was good reason, therefore, for a man's learning to depend upon his own courage and strength and skill. He had nothing else to protect him, whether he was good or bad. In the typical days of the Western bad man, life was the property of the individual, and not of society, and one man placed his life against another's as the only way of solving hard personal problems. Those days and those conditions brought out some of the boldest and most reckless men the earth ever saw. Before we freely criticize them, we ought fully to understand them.

Maurice G. Fulton
APOCRYPHA OF BILLY THE KID

This early study of Billy the Kid from the Las Vegas Optic *is one of the first tries to paint Billy as he appeared and sounded. The author, Maurice Fulton, was one of the first academics to concern himself with Billy the Kid's story. His contributions to the folklore, history, and literature on the subject are enormous. His* Maurice G. Fulton's History of the Lincoln County War *is one of the landmark works on the history of the Southwest. This piece has been excerpted from* Folk-Say, A Regional Miscellany, *1930.*

FROM
FOLK-SAY
A Regional Miscellany

edited by B. A. Botkin
1930

————•◦•————

ardly had the young outlaw and noted desperado of the Pecos country, William H. Bonney (whose real name has grown nearly obsolescent in the face of his popular pseudonym Billy the Kid), received his quietus from Pat Garrett's revolver in July, 1881, at Fort Sumner, New Mexico, than his career became the target for exaggeration and riotous imaginings. The folk mind, even then avid for details, was ready to gulp down whatever might be offered. In a highly uncritical mood, it accepted whatever might substantiate its two leading notions anent this "darling of the common people": first, that "he was the worst bad man that ever strapped on a six-shooter in the West"; and secondly, that "he had killed a man for every year of his life, not including Mexicans and Indians."

Such fabricating was going on so fast and furious that it moved to disgust Pat Garrett, the former friend and associate of the Kid's, to whom had come in the course of time the sheriff-ship of Lincoln County and the task of hunting down the young ruffian which had finally eventuated in "capturing him by killing him." To promulgate more of a plain and unvarnished account, Pat Garrett enlisted the aid of Ash Upson, a rolling stone of the old West who had been a newspaper man in his Eastern days and who was now come to a standstill in the infant settlement of Roswell, New Mexico, where Pat Garrett was then living. In several ways Ash Upson was suited to become Pat Garrett's coadjutor. He not only had some facility in clothing his material in the florid journalese of that generation, but he claimed first-hand knowledge of the Kid's earlier life, acquired while he was a boarder in the home of the Kid's mother at different places in New Mexico.

The outcome of this literary partnership was the so-called "Pat Garrett's Life of Billy the Kid," which, as the preface avouched, was an attempt at an authentic account in order "to correct the thousand false statements which have appeared in the newspapers and in yellow-covered cheap novels." The authors also went on to state that "of the latter no less than three have been foisted upon the public, any one of which might have been the history of any other outlaw who ever lived, but which was miles from correct as applied to the Kid. These pretend to disclose his name, the place of his nativity, the particulars of his career, the circumstances which drove him to his desperate life, detailing a hundred deeds of reckless crime of which he was never guilty and in localities which he never visited."

II

I have never been able to discover a single one of these accounts of the Kid prior to the Garrett-Upson pamphlet, which was published towards the close of 1882 by the Santa Fé *New Mexican* press. But I am inclined to believe I have found a few chapters from one of them in some stray copies of the Las Vegas *Optic.* In the latter part of 1882, that newspaper ran in chapter installments what purported to be an account of the Kid and may have been a sample of the attempts at biography which so moved the indignation of Pat Garrett. I do not have the least inkling who wrote the hotchpotch, nor do I know whether it had separate publication as a book or pamphlet. The earlier installments are missing, but fortunately the latter ones have a consecutiveness that develop them into almost a complete resumé of the Kid's career. Despite this incompleteness, the excerpts may have some value in illustrating the beginnings of the prolific legendizing that has gone on for nearly fifty years and is still going on, both in print and in oral tradition.

In the account, the narrator is represented as having been a visitor at the rendezvous of the Kid and his gang. While there he becomes acquainted with the Kid's history, largely through the stilted device of investigative questions. This is shown in Chapter VII, the first of those I reproduce.

BILLY'S STORY OF HIS LIFE

"A penny for your thoughts, did you say?" I asked, arising and rubbing my eyes; "you can have them for less money, Mr. William Antrim."

Billy the Kid started perceptibly. "So you know my name?" he said at length.

"Yes, Billy, I know your name."

"And how much more do you know about me?"

"Very little more."

"And that little?"

"Is purely hearsay. Of course your name is not Antrim."

"Certainly not. And you said it was because you knew that this was not my name?"

"Precisely."

"And your object?"

"Simply to induce you to tell me your story."

"Simply that?"

"Assuredly; nothing more."

"And you would really like to hear my story?"

"I really would."

"Then you shall; but first you must answer me a few questions."

"With pleasure."

"How did you know that my name was Antrim?"

"Is it not the name under which you registered at the county jail of Grant county?"

He bit his lip as he replied: "It is."

"I ask your pardon; I meant no offence; you asked me a question, and I answered it."

"You did right. Did you know me as Billy the Kid last night in Dempsey's?"

"I did."

"How did you learn it?"

"I was told by a man you once went through on the road."

"Paddy O'Shaughnesey?"

"Yes."

"Well, you imagined right. I would have done so only for you. But weren't you afraid of me?"

"No. I had done nothing to harm you."

"That is true; but for all that you ran a risk."

"I know I did."

"Why did you do so?"

"Because I like Dempsey."

"Why do you like him?"

"He has proved himself my friend."

"Well, well! that is enough. Now then I like you, and I'd like to have you join my band. We lead a pretty independent life, and as a general thing we have everything we want. Our band is a large one, and we have nothing to fear. What do you say? Will you join us?"

"I could not answer that question at once without first telling you a long commonplace story, and before doing that, I would be glad if you tell me your own story. It must need some terrible motive to induce a man to redden his hands with the blood of fellow beings as frequently as you have done."

Billy the Kid's brow grew black, and for one moment I feared he meditated an assault upon me. But such was not the case.

"You are right," he said at last. "I have a motive, and a terrible one. There are very few who know my story—only three in all my band whom I have trusted with the whole of it. There are a good many persons who fancy they know all about me, yet who, in reality, know next to nothing at all.

"I was born in County Limerick, Ireland, about 1859. My father's name was Williams. He was a poor Irish peasant, and like all the poor classes of peasantry suffered much and did not escape persecution. I don't like to dwell on those days. They were too bitter. What finally drove me away from there was the ruin of my two sisters by a son of our landlord. My father vowed vengeance against him, and the gay young villain succeeded in having the poor old man arrested on a trumpery charge and lodged in jail, where, in a few weeks he died from the effects of bad treatment and a broken heart. This decided my poor mother, and she took passage from Cork to Canada, bringing with her myself and my unfortunate sisters. From Montreal we went to Nova Scotia, and the girls were so lucky as to get good positions in service. My mother was less fortunate, for, in about a year's time, she allowed herself to be persuaded into marrying an old reprobate named Antrim, and soon afterward accompanied him to New Mexico. This was in 1869. After many changes the family brought up in Silver City, and it was here that I was destined to begin a career, which, had I received proper treatment from others, I should never have adopted."

Chapter VIII is missing from the numbers of the *Optic* that have come into my hands, and I am forced to confess a gap before continuing the story with Chapter IX.

MORE HORRIBLE ADVENTURES

"So," I observed, "it is to yourself that you owe your striking patronymic?"

"To myself! and if I do say it, the handle has fitted me right well."

"How did you and the landlord get along?"

"First rate, for about a week; and if I had had no one but him to deal with, everything would have gone well enough. But the women folks kind of soured on me, and I didn't hanker after kitchen work anyhow. When I'd been there a few days, I helped myself to a keg of butter and sold it to a Chinaman. I might have known better. Never trust one of those heathen devils. The first thing he did was to go up to the hotel and give me away."

"How did you get out of it?"

"Oh, I bamboozled the landlord into the belief that I was very sorry for what I had done, and he consented to deduct the price of the butter from my wages and let the matter drop.

"But I only took this course to gain time. Ten dollars a month was too small potatoes for me anyhow without paying for a twenty-dollar keg of butter. But I meant to freeze this until I could do something better.

"Not long after this I had a chance, as I thought, to crib the overcoat of the infernal Chinaman who had given me away on this butter business. I got his coat, but he dropped to the racket, and went out and had me arrested.

"Then the landlord got mad, and said he'd have nothing more to do with me. I saw the jig was up, and that I'd be put to it to take care of myself. I resolved to lie shady, and wait for something to turn up.

"When my trial came up, I pleaded guilty. Of course I was convicted, and they shoved a year's sentence on me. I began to work it out in the most lamb-like manner possible, and before very long I had hoodwinked my jailers out of all suspicion. But all the while I was looking out for a chance of escape.

"The first place I looked at was the chimney, but it was so small that at the start I gave up all thought of it. Yet there seemed to be no other outlet to the uncomfortable place. If I had had a knife or file it would have been an easy matter to have got out. But I had nothing. Escape I must, for I would rather have died than stayed there.

"So I resolved to try the chimney anyhow, although I knew that if I was caught, they would use me pretty roughly. I tried it that night. It was a tight squeeze and took me over an hour. But I got out."

"I heard afterwards that the sheriff was the most amazed man in the Territory when he found out I was gone. The chimney, as he remarked himself, was so small he could hardly put his foot into the hole.

"I cannot express to you the joy I experienced at finding myself free, but this feeling was quickly succeeded by one of hate for the G—d d—n Chinaman who had put me to so much trouble."

I looked up in surprise. It was the first time I had heard Billy the Kid make use of an oath. It is a very common mistake to suppose that all border ruffians interlard their remarks with oaths. Not that they are any too good to employ such expressions, or that they never do. But they use them, they believe, not for ornament but for emphasis.

The Kid noticed my surprise.

"Do you wonder at my feelings?" he asked.

"Not at all," I replied, "but I was astonished to hear you swear."

"I astonish myself that way sometimes," he said almost sheepishly, "but I say just what I mean when I say 'G—d d—n the ugly Chinaman!'"

"Very well," I rejoined, "go on with the story."

Billy the Kid resumed: "My rage against him was tremendous, and I resolved to put him out of the way of ever playing another mean trick on a white man.

"I went to his cabin and peered through the open door. He was alone and asleep. It was necessary to work quickly. Any noise and I might be retaken. I stole to his side and cut his throat from ear to ear."

In spite of myself, I shivered in terror at this cool, almost demoniacal narrative.

CHAPTER X
END OF BILLY THE KID'S STORY

"It was my first murder," continued Billy the Kid, calmly refilling his pipe. "I acknowledge that at first I felt a little scared at what I had done; but I had no time for reflection. It was necessary for me to get out of Silver City in the most lively manner possible.

"The Chinaman had a good horse, and I helped myself to it and lit out for Arizona. I knew that I stood a pretty good chance of escape. In the first place, it would be long after daylight before I would be missed from the jail.

"Again, the Chinaman being dead could not complain of the loss of his horse, and the chances were that he would not himself be missed by any one for a day or two at least. And by that time all trace of my trail would have been lost.

"I wandered on through the country, meeting with no especial adventure, until I came to the border of Arizona. There I stumbled into a small village which boasted of a small blacksmith shop. The blacksmith engaged me as a helper in his establishment.

"I did not care a straw about the wages he proposed to pay me, but I thought (and I thought truly) that some knowledge of the trade would be of some service to me. Besides, I wanted to gain some information about the land in that part of the country.

"Things would have gone on pleasantly if the blacksmith had been a decent sort of fellow. Every one else about the place was kind and civil enough, but this fellow was an ugly drunken brute whom nobody could get along with.

"He was a bully by nature, and he tried in every way to impose on me. I suppose he thought that because I was mild-looking and mild-mannered that he could ride over me roughshod.

"But that didn't go down with me. I don't take any stock in the fisticuff business. You simply get a skin peppering, and it spoils your beauty. Stand a man as along as you can; then, if he don't suit you, kill him."

"What!" I said nervously.

Billy the Kid laughed. "Certainly, my dear sir," said he. "Take the case of this blacksmith for instance. Will you dare tell me I did not do right?"

"Why! did you kill him?" I asked.

"I did, for a fact," he answered, "and why not?

"You see," he continued without waiting for me to reply, "this drunken beast was very fond of amusing himself with me. He liked to throw pieces of iron at me 'just to see if his aim was good,' as he said himself.

"I didn't mind much; I was there for a purpose, and it didn't make any difference to me as long as the old fellow did not really hurt me. But one day he took his pincers and pulled a red-hot horseshoe from the fire. Turning around, he flung it at me. I dodged, but it fell on my right arm, burning it pretty severely.

"It made me writhe with pain, and, as though to increase my torture, that infernal old fiend fairly danced up and down, rubbing his hands and exulting in my pain.

"I said nothing, but I went to the house and prepared a plaster of flour and molasses, which I bound upon my arm as carefully as possible. Then I went out and saddled my horse, throwing over the saddle my only property, a couple of blankets.

"I visited the blacksmith's room and helped myself to his rifle, a pair of revolvers, and a fine bowie knife, together with all the cartridges I could find.

"After this, I mounted my horse and rode to the door of the blacksmith's shop. 'Hello,' I shouted.

"'Here, you young devil! see what this man wants!' he ordered, imagining I was around the place.

"Not seeing me, he came out, and I immediately shot him through the heart."

CHAPTER XI
THE END OF IT ALL

"It is getting on towards morning," said Billy the Kid, "and my boys will soon be back. It will not do for me to talk to you before them. So I must cut my story short. Besides, as soon as they get here, I must run you back in sight of Santa Fé."

"Good," I exclaimed, "we can talk it out on the way."

"Not at all," he replied, "eyes for the prairies and the hills, ears for the slightest sound. No distracting your ears by chin music."

"Very good," I complied, "let us hear the whole story now."

So he began to "boil it down" in a very lively fashion.

"I knew I had to run for it, and I did. And I beat them in the race. I laid low for two years, not having any very exciting sport, but getting a band of boys together. My two murders had made me reckless, and I no longer hesitated at taking life.

"At the end of two years the Lincoln County War began, and I thought I might as well have a finger in the pie. A short time before a man died, leaving about $12,000 behind him for the benefit of his heirs. A woman who said she was his only sister came to New Mexico determined she would get hold of the cash, but in the meanwhile the administrator of the estate was trying to gobble the whole thing for his own benefit. I hated to see the quarrel going on, and made up my mind I would have that money for my own use. The sheriff of the county took the part of the administrator, and some of the rough element sided with him. But my band gave them a tough tussle, and I killed thirteen of them myself before the thing was ended. The sheriff was among them. I cooked his goose one day when he was making an attack on a house in which I and some of my friends were concealed.

"They elected a new sheriff, and not long after they run me down at a house in the town and put me in the county jail. They had two big ruffians to stand guard over me, who had fought against me and my band. These same men were murderers of note, and that, of course, made them just the right kind of fellows to watch over me. They condemned me to be hung, but I gave them the slip. They had me ironed, hands and ankles, with a heavy ball attached to the anklets. When the day for the hanging drew near, I induced one of the watchers to unloosen one of my handcuffs so that I might eat with more ease. He did so, but I took no advantage of it until two days before the day appointed for my execution. That day one of the guards went to town to fill his whisky jug. I got the other fellow to talking, and getting up behind him, I raised my hand holding the two handcuffs, and hit him on the head, dropping him like an ox. Before he could rise, I relieved him of his pistols and sent a ball nearly through his head. I then went into the guard room, and loading all the rifles took them to a room which overlooked the road to the town.

"The guard who had gone after whisky had heard me when I fired the shot that killed his comrade, and suspecting something was wrong, came running up the road just as I opened the window. I grasped a rifle, and when he got within hailing distance, I said, 'Hello, Bill!' He looked up, and instantly I shot him through the heart.

"I then jumped out of the window and threatened the cook with immediate death if he did not catch the best horse he could find and bring him to the prison. By this time a crowd began to gather, but no one offered to lay a hand on me. The cook got a horse which I mounted, but the brute threw me. The cook caught the horse again, and this time I stuck to him and rode away. Since that I have kept pretty shady."

"I should think you'd need to," I remarked.

Billy the Kid laughed. "Get up now," he said, "and eat. I must see you back to Santa Fé."

Back to Santa Fé we soon started, and arrived within a mile of the town a little after nightfall.

"Good-by," said the Kid, holding out his hand, "and don't forget me when you're gone."

"That I'll not," I said heartily shaking hands with him.

"Take this," he said, holding out a beautiful revolver, "and keep it to remember Billy the Kid."

He pressed the spurs in his horse's side and sped swiftly away.

I rode into the town. Dempsey had disappeared. I left Santa Fé, and went to the City of Mexico, from which place I have just returned.

A few days ago I saw a sketch of Billy the Kid, describing his death. He had reached the end of his tether. I felt sorry in spite of myself. He was a brave man and might have been powerful for good had his early training been a proper one. Alas! this is one of the myriads of "might have beens."

III

Such was the way a writer of a penny-dreadful in 1882 converted his modicum of truth into what would give the readers of that generation the desired thrill. Most of the recent writings about the Kid exhibit much the same procedure, it may be observed. The blessings of gullibility have been extolled by no less a philosophic mind than Carlyle's, and mankind's general willingness to undergo imposture, nay, its yearning for it rather than authenticated fact, is nowhere more in evidence than in the case of its popular heroes, be they reputable or disreputable. The vagaries of popular psychology are not to be gainsaid, however much some of us may desire rather more of "crude fact" even when we read about the hard cases and tough customers of frontier times.

J. Frank Dobie
A VAQUERO OF THE BRUSH COUNTRY

*Frank Dobie was a writer, historian, and folklorist in the rich tradi-
tions of Texas and the Southwest. He had an ear for a good story.
In this piece from an early work, he examines Billy the Kid and the
bad-man tradition in American literature. Going against the grain of
many other period attempts to characterize Billy the Kid, he finds little
resemblance to Robin Hood.*

*Dobie was for many years the secretary-editor of the Texas Folk-
lore Society. He was instrumental in saving the Texas longhorn from
extinction and made the same efforts toward preservation on behalf of
many a story of the old Southwest. His other well-known books include*
Coronado's Children, Apache Gold and Yaqui Silver, *and* Tales
of Old Time Texas.

A VAQUERO OF THE BRUSH COUNTRY

By J. Frank Dobie
Partly from the Reminiscences of John Young
1943

———————

But to get back to the business of the "cowboy detective"—and I was a year ahead of Charlie Siringo in playing detective on Billy the Kid. About the first thing I saw after I got well into the Dorsey range was a bunch of old F O S cows; I found that they were scattered all over the country. The sight of them made me feel at home, for the F O S brand belonged to Frank Skidmore in South Texas. I had branded many a calf for him and brought a goodly number of his animals out of the brush west of the Nueces. Dorsey had bought a big string of cows from Skidmore and they had been driven up the Goodnight-Loving Trail. He gave me a letter addressed to the officer in charge of Fort Union, telling me that I should read it. It merely stated that the bearer was in the employ of the writer, that no questions were to be asked of me, and that any request I made was to be granted, even to the use of soldiers. The words "U.S. Senator" were at the tail end of the signature.

From Dorsey's ranch I went on to headquarters for Hall Brothers on the Dry Cimarron. There the Halls gave me two letters, one to a ranchman in New Mexico named Cameron and one to another ranchman farther on named Lewellyn. Each letter contained a statement of my mission and a request for aid and secrecy. I exchanged Payaso for a little Spanish pony that looked like something the cats had dragged in, exchanged my new Frazier saddle for an old hull patched with rawhide, hung up my prized Stetson hat and in its place put on an old floppy piece of headgear that even a Kansas nester would have been ashamed to wear. Then I announced that my name was no longer John Young but A. M. Rider—and I hit the rocks for Turkey Mountain. The A. M. in my assumed name stood for "A Mule," and I was the Rider. My plan was to look for some kind of job that would allow me to watch what was going on. Only one thing worried me—that flop hat, which always signifies slouchiness and not infrequently an unfurnished upper story. Oliver Wendell Holmes summed up the cowboy point of view when he wrote:

> Wear a good hat. The secret of good looks
> Lies with the beavers in Canadian brooks.

I'll say right here that the little Spanish pony I set out on— with a detailed map of Mexico branded into his shoulders, his hips, and his thighs on both sides—belied his outward appearance. He had a bottom that no amount of riding could plumb, and he was a whirlwind after a cow. I named him Whirlwind.

At the end of the third day I unsaddled Whirlwind in the corral back of the Cameron ranch house. I found Mr. Cameron to be a fatherly old Scotchman; and after he had read the letter addressed to him and we had eaten supper and were sitting alone in front of his roaring fire, he fairly exuded canny information and beneficent caution. He warned me that I was in a country where the slightest suspicion of my business on the part of the rustlers would put a bullet through my back, for they were "positively the most cold-blooded gang of men in the West."

"You have heard, young man," Mr. Cameron went on, "that 'there is no law west of the Pecos.' You have heard the truth, and the most lawless and the most murderous outlaw of the trans-Pecos country is Billy the Kid—the man you have come to spy on. You do not know him, you cannot know him as I know him. Do not speak his name. You cannot tell when you are speaking to a friend of his or an enemy. If a man is his friend he dares not mention the fact; if a man is his enemy, he is even more silent.

Such talk naturally led me to confide to Mr. Cameron that I had another letter, similar to the one just delivered, addressed to a Mr. Lewellyn farther down the trail. When I told him about this letter, Mr. Cameron was silent for a long time while he gazed into the fire. Then he spoke.

"If you will take my advice," he said, "I will save your life."

I was ready to trust him and told him that I was relying absolutely on what he said.

"Then," he replied, "throw that other letter into the fire. The Halls thought that they were aiding you when they wrote it, but they do not know their man. Throw the letter into the fire. To deliver it would be like firing a pistol into your own brains."

Without a word I pitched the letter into the fire. I subsequently visited the Lewellyn ranch and when I saw the layout that Lewellyn had around him I was profoundly thankful that the letter was in ashes. My Guardian Angel had once again saved me.

After the letter was burned Mr. Cameron told me the full story of Billy the Kid. In general it followed the accounts that have since been made familiar to the world by Pat Garrett, Walter Noble Burns, and other biographers of the notorious outlaw. I shall repeat only such parts as relate directly to Mr. Cameron's and my own experiences. I cannot vouch for the accuracy of all the details. According to Mr. Cameron, Antrim, the step-father of William Bonney (Billy the Kid), Mrs. Antrim, and the boy, had several years before come by his ranch in an ox wagon; there a snowstorm held them for several days, and during this time Cameron became fairly familiar with the family and their past. They were looking for a place to locate, and he advised them to open a restaurant at Fort Union, a few miles on down the old Santa Fé trail.

The Antrims set up a restaurant at Fort Union, and for a while the boy, Billy, waited on the table[s], making friends of the cowboys, who patronized the place liberally and took to calling their waiter "Billy the Kid." Now there were a lot of negro soldiers at Fort Union and soon they were calling the boy "Billy the Goat," or simply "Billy Goat." Sometimes when Billy passed these negroes they would bleat at him in the manner of a goat. Such teasing did not sit well with his proud disposition, although he liked the name the cowboys had given him. One day when a negro soldier bleated at Billy, Billy threw a rock at his tormentor. The negro went for a gun and so did Billy. As a result there was one less negro for the government to support and Billy the Kid was fairly launched on his man-killing career. Before he became a really bad man, however, Mr. Cameron kept him on the ranch for a while, employing him as a cowboy.

Skipping the murders of Indians and Mexicans and the various killings connected with the Lincoln County War, we find Billy the Kid next refusing to trust himself to Governor Lew Wallace, who offered amnesty if Billy would give himself up to the courts. Instead of surrendering, the Kid rode with five men through the Turkey Mountains and across the Plains to an Indian camp, where they stole a bunch of horses. They sold the horses on the Canadian, the gang split up, and the Kid, with Tom O'Phalliard and Charlie Bowdre accompanying him, went to Tascosa to make an alliance with some buffalo hunters. He had discovered a new field for operations. He had found cattle on the Canadian to steal and tie-cutters and railroad-graders to buy them.

It just happened that I had entered Tascosa at the time he was beginning operations on the Canadian, though I did not then know anything about him and had no interest in his affairs.

I rode away from the Cameron ranch with a much firmer comprehension of affairs than I had when I rode up to it. When I got to Fort Union I presented Senator Dorsey's letter to the commanding officer. He looked at me in my flop hat, looked at Whirlwind and looked at the letter again. Finally he said, "The fort is yours." As matters turned out, I had no occasion to command the fort, but the welcome was reassuring. From Fort Union I went directly to the grading camp on the Canadian River and there got a job herding the beef cattle that the contractors were buying from rustlers.

Beyond all doubt the cattle were stolen cattle, but none of them bore the brands I represented. During the course of my employment I helped the contractors purchase several small bunches of cattle, all of them from rustlers; but evidently the thieves were not bothering stock belonging to the Cimarron Cattle Raisers' Association. If they were depredating on stock north of the Canadian I never heard of it. My job was a sinecure. I kept the cattle in a pen at night and during the daytime I would frequently leave them to graze in sight of a saloon where I spent long hours among the rustlers, from whom, however, I learned little, as they were a tight-lipped crew. Twice I saw Billy the Kid and recognized him as one of the men I had treated in the saloon at Tascosa; I did not form any acquaintance with him. One evening I settled with my employers and, without saying I had quit, rode away. By daylight Whirlwind and I were forty miles north on the route to the Dry Cimarron. And so *adios* to Billy the Kid.

What was there about this killer of men, this pariah of society, this product of Bowery slum and Western lawlessness that has made him the object of such wide and undimming interest? He has been the subject of half a dozen biographies— one of them by Pat Garrett, the man who killed him, and now Pat Garrett's book has been revived and annotated by a college professor. In the Pecos country legendary tales concerning him are as numerous as legendary tales concerning Sam Houston are in East Texas and Tennessee. A monument marking his burial place at Fort Sumner has been proposed. Whereas once his purported "trigger finger" was exhibited for two bits a peep, Philip Leloir's bully ballad of "The Finger of Billy the Kid" is now read in public libraries, and in ten thousand homes and drug stores the phonograph wails out a dolorous folk song of the Kid's deeds and death.

> I'll sing you a true song of Billy the Kid,
> I'll sing of the desperate deeds that he did,
> Way out in New Mexico long, long ago
> When a man's only chance was his own fo'ty-fo'.

When Billy the Kid was a very young lad
In old Silver City he went to the bad;
Way out in the West with a gun in his hand
At the age of twelve years there he killed his first man.

Fair Mexican maidens play guitars and sing
A song about Billy, their boy bandit king,
How ere his young manhood had reached its bad end
He had a notch on his pistol for twenty-one men.

'Twas on the same night that poor Billy died,
He said to his friends: "I'm not satisfied.
There are twenty-one men I have put bullets through
And Sheriff Pat Garrett must make twenty-two."

Now, this is how Billy the Kid met his fate:
The bright moon was shining, the hour was late.
Shot down by Pat Garrett, who once was his friend,
The young outlaw's life had now come to its end.

There's many a man with a face fine and fair
Who starts out in the life with a chance to be square,
But just like poor Billy he wanders astray
And loses his life in the very same way.

Billy the Kid "was the Fairy Prince of New Mexico,"
sentimentalizes Kyle S. Crichton, the charming and exuberant
biographer of another New Mexican hero, Elfego Baca. "The
Robin Hood of New Mexico," shouts Walter Noble Burns, who

has just made something of a reputation of his *Saga of Billy the Kid*. Even that fine English gentleman, seasoned scholar, and gallant adventurer, R. B. Townshend, whose *The Tenderfoot in New Mexico* should become a classic in the literature of the West, was, after a personal encounter with the Kid, inclined to regard him as "a mitigated ruffian" of delightful humor. Charlie Siringo, who led an expedition of cowboys in an attempt to recover cattle that the Kid had stolen, relates how when the outfit heard that Billy had killed two guards and escaped hanging, one of the men yelled, "Hurrah for Billy the Kid!" and dived into the Pecos with his boots on. Sheriff Pat Garrett, who in writing his *Authentic Life of Billy, the Kid* had the advantage over all other biographers of knowing his hero personally, seems to have been strangely attracted by "his pleasant manners and openhanded generosity" and he proposed to "dissever the Kid's memory from that of meaner villains whose deeds have been attributed to him."

On the other hand, upright and clear-eyed peace officers like James B. Gillett and the law abiding, virtue preserving, though not generally imagination cultivating, citizens who give New Mexico its stamina are apt to regard all laudations and condonements of the West's most spectacular outlaw with disgust. To such people the Kid was a stark murderer and a mean thief. As a matter of history the Kid was a professional gambler, a professional thief, and a professional gunman. He was never much of a cowboy and he cannot at all be classed as "a cowboy gone wrong." He gambled with negroes; he cheated Mexicans; he helped to ambush and murder three Apache Indians for their store of pelts and blankets. His followers were for the most part ignorant, sordid, vicious toughs. As for the polished Don Juan figure that more than one journalist has sought to mould him into, the only basis for this conception seems to be the fact that a few Mexican girls of the *pelado* class danced with him. However much may be made of his loyalty to his friends, the truth remains that he shot in the back one man who had been his friend. When his "right bower," Charlie Bowdre, dying from a bullet wound, staggered into the hut where Billy the Kid and his crew were besieged, the Kid shoved him out again with these words: "They've got you, Charlie. You're about done for. Go out and see if you can't kill one of those sons-of-bitches before you die." As to the end of the outlaw's life, he had warned Sheriff Garrett that he would shoot him on sight. There would be, there could be, no quarter on either side. According to all laws that govern such business, Pat Garrett shot Billy the Kid honorably, justly, and wisely. There have been honorable and noble and admirable outlaws *against tyranny and injustice,* like Rob Roy, like Wallace and Bruce, like Dull Knife, the great Cheyenne warrior; but when measured alongside such men as these, Billy the Kid appears tawdry.

It's not the "writer fellers" with their talk of "Robin Hood" and "the Fairy Prince" who keep the memory of Billy the Kid alive in the Kid's own country. It's the men who have themselves ridden the blood-spattered trails that Billy rode. Mostly the tales of these men are impersonal without suggestion of glorification; mostly also they are unverifiable. Sometimes the tales get into print, as the persistent one about Billy the Kid's being alive today and in hiding among the Mogollon Mountains, or down in Guadalajara, Mexico, or somewhere else. In 1926 a book of reminiscences called *Frontier Dust,* by a loose-memoried old timer, John Lord, came out of Hartford, Connecticut, and in this book is an excellent example of the apocryphal tales that circulate so freely to keep Billy the Kid's memory fresh.

"Billy was working for Chisholm [Chisum]," says Mr. Lord. "He and the camp cook got into a row. The cook had a frying pan on the fire with a lot of hot grease in it. He grabbed it and either struck or threw it at Billy and some of the grease burned the Kid severely. Billy didn't do a thing but jerk out his pistol and kill the cook—got on his horse and rode away, an outlaw."

Bill Cole of Valentine, Texas, is fond of telling this anecdote—an example of scores of other anecdotes that have never been printed. One time a Texas cowboy named Dave Martin was riding from somewhere west of the Pecos to old Fort Concho, now San Angelo. He crossed the Pecos a little while before sundown, intending to stake his horse and stay all night at the deserted ruins of Fort Lancaster. When he got to the old chimneys he saw a rider coming west. The two men met, greeted each other, and both unsaddled and ate supper. The rider going west had no blanket, and Dave suggested that they make their beds together, for Dave was leading a packhorse loaded with bed roll. As the men were pulling off their boots the stranger said:

"By the way, if you have occasion to get up in the night be sure to nudge me and wake me up before you stir around any. I might wake up suddenly and shoot if I detected a man walking up to our bed."

"Well, I'll shore [sic] wake you up before I get out of bed," Dave replied laughing.

"You're going to Fort Concho, did you say?" the stranger went on.

"Yes."

"Well, when you get there you'll see my mark. I'm Billy the Kid."

At daybreak the men parted, Dave Martin going on east and his cautious bedfellow going on west. When two days later Dave got to Fort Concho, Billy the Kid's "mark" had been put under ground but there was plenty of talk about both mark and marksmanship. The mark consisted of two men who had worked for John Chisum, victims of the Lincoln County feud.

When the Kid was tried in Mesilla for the killing of Sheriff Brady and found guilty, the judge of the court, so a floating story goes, pronounced the death sentence with a gathering emphasis that was highly elocutionary.

"I do hereby sentence you to be hanged by the neck," he intoned, "until you are dead! dead!! dead!!!"

"Yes," Billy the Kid calmly retorted, looking the judge straight in the eyes, "yes, and you can go to hell! hell!! hell!!!"

So much are relics of Billy the Kid prized and talked about that Charlie Siringo said "it would be a safe gamble to bet that there are a wagon load" of pistols purporting to have belonged to him "scattered over the United States." At the meeting of the trail drivers in San Antonio in October, 1928, Gus Gildea of Arizona told a group of men, not without pride, that he and Billy fought in opposite ranks during [the] New Mexico troubles for three years with a gentlemen's agreement that neither of them would shoot the other.

Thus the Kid's trigger finger goes shooting on. After all, Billy the Kid was more than a common killer and thief, more than a common leech on society. He was an uncommon killer, he was an uncommon thief. He had something in him that has called to the imagination not only of writers but of the people at large. He was indisputably brave and he was, in his own sphere, absolutely supreme. In preserving his own life and in taking the lives of his hunters he was a sheer genius. He was as single-minded in this business and as economical as Napoleon; hence his hard way with the dying Charlie Bowdre. He was probably the quickest and surest man on the trigger anywhere south or west of Wild Bill Hickok. His nerve never broke; his alertness never wavered; his determination never flagged. He had extraordinary personal magnetism, for without personal magnetism a mere boy could never have led and held in check a gang of hard, seasoned men. He controlled himself as well as he controlled others; never impetuous, he deliberated every act, every robbery, every murder. Although revengeful, he was generous hearted—particularly generous with property that belonged to other people—and, being generous hearted, he had a certain winsome care-freeness. Above all, he possessed to an unusual degree what Mirabeau finely called "the art of daring." Because he possessed this "art of daring," because his daring apotheosized youth—youth in the saddle—youth with a flaming gun—and because his daring kept him running and balancing on the edge of a frightful precipice, as it were, for an unprecedented length of time, Billy the Kid will always be interesting, will always appeal to the popular imagination. Despite facts, he seems on the way to become the Robin Hood, the Fairy Prince not only of New Mexico but of the Old West.

JEFF C. DYKES
BILLY THE KID WAS MY FRIEND

*Jeff C. Dykes was an old-time bibliographer, critic, and bookseller—
an all-around "bookman" of the sort almost never seen anymore. His
particular specialty was Western titles. Here Dykes expertly evaluates
the accounts of those who encountered Billy the Kid in their own travels through the West. First-person accounts are among the most sought
after by historians, but are often the most unreliable. Dykes's good book
sense shows us which was which.*

Dykes's well-known works include Fifty Great Western Illustra-
tors *(1975) and* Billy the Kid: Bibliography of a Legend *(1952).
This excerpt is taken from* Western High Spots: Reading and Collecting Guides.

WESTERN HIGH SPOTS
Reading and Collecting Guides

By Jeff C. Dykes
1977

———•◦•———

I t seems that most of the old-timers who told or wrote of their
experiences in the Pecos Valley of New Mexico, or the Texas
Panhandle, in the late 1870s knew William H. Bonney, better
known as Billy the Kid. Of well over sixty personal narratives
of these old-timers included in my Kid bibliographical check
list, only three come to mind that do not include a claim
that the narrator was personally acquainted with the little
outlaw. Teddy Blue, Ike Fridge and J. L. Hill told of the Kid
but admitted their tales were hearsay only. Of course, not all
the narrators introduced the subject of the boy desperado
with the statement, "Billy the Kid was my friend." There were
variations—"The Kid was my buddy"; "The Kid was drinking at
the bar when I rode up"; "Billy was a Chisum hand when I went
to work for Uncle John"; and many others including, "I saved
Billy the Kid's life."

Most personal narratives defy classification—that is,
particularly when told or set down half a century after the
events described, it is difficult to say they are either fact or
fiction. More often they are a combination of both—fact
limited by time-dimmed memory, and tempered with camp-fire
and barroom tales, folk legends and hearsay. A clear majority,

I believe, can be described as "tall tales" and as such, belong to the field of folklore rather than history.

Perhaps you have accepted the flat statement made by practically every historian that Billy was born in New York City (some say Brooklyn) in 1859. There is at least one dissenter— Deadwood Dick, in his book *The Life and Adventures of Nat Love*, claims that he met the Kid at Holbrook, Arizona, in the fall of 1880 and that they rode to Silver City together. Near Silver City the Kid pointed out the log cabin where he was born. Dick also states that he arrived at Fort Sumner the very night the Kid was killed—Billy "was laying dead at Pete Maxwell's ranch." Nice timing!

THE KID'S FIRST VICTIM

Or perhaps you have long accepted Pat Garrett's version of the killing of the burly ruffian who had insulted Billy's mother as his first act of violence. Perhaps it would be more accurate to call it Ash Upson's version, since William A. Keleher offers strong evidence in his excellent book, *The Fabulous Frontier,* that the entire volume was written by the pioneer newspaper man. You remember the story—the insult, the saving of the boy from a bad beating at the hands of the ruffian by Ed Moulton, and the knifing of the ruffian as he was about to strike Moulton with a heavy chair during a barroom fight. "Once, twice, thrice his arm rose and fell. Then rushing through the crowd, his right hand above his head grasping a pocketknife, blade dripping with blood, he went out into the night, an outcast and a wanderer, a murderer self-baptized in blood." Billy was "about twelve" at the time.

Pat's, or Ash's, version has been widely accepted and much copied. Certainly, it is a romantic enough beginning of a killer's career but a good many of the old-timers tell it differently.

For example, Mrs. Edith M. Bowyer in *Observations of a Ranchwoman in New Mexico* (London, 1898), repeats the story as she heard it in the Mesilla Valley in the early 1890s. A young dishwasher is ill-used by a big burly man cook in one of the towns of the territory. The dishwasher wounds the bully with a pistol shot and flees the town. He turns up some days later, half-starved, at Morton's (Tunstall's) ranch. The dishwasher is the Kid and he repays the kind Englishman for his care and protection with a passionate devotion.

John Lord has a different version of a cook being the Kid's first victim. In *Frontier Dust* he states that the Kid was working for John Chisholm (Chisum) and got in an argument with the camp cook. The enraged cook threw some hot grease on Billy and, of course, Billy jerked out his gun and killed the cook. He rode away an outlaw.

As Ike Fridge told the story to Jodie D. Smith (*History of the Chisum War, or, Life of Ike Fridge*), Billy visited a Mexican sheep herder's camp. He prepared a meal, and when the Mexican returned and objected, the Kid killed him. Reason? "Self-defense"—the Mexican ran at him with a knife.

Fred E. Sutton in his reminiscences in *The Trail Drivers of Texas* uses the old dime novel story of the Kid knifing a boy companion to death in New York City. This version of the beginning of the Kid's career also appeared (perhaps first appeared), in a brief article in *The National Police Gazette*, August 13, 1881.

As John Young told the story to J. Frank Dobie (*A Vaquero of the Brush Country*), the Antrims (Billy's mother and step-father) had a restaurant at Fort Union, and Billy helped as a waiter. The cowboys nicknamed the boy "Billy the Kid." He liked the name but not the corruptions of it such as "Billy the Goat," used by the negro soldiers stationed at Fort Union. They also "bleated" at him as he passed, and on one occasion the proud boy threw a rock at one of his tormentors. The soldier went for a gun and so did Billy—result? One less soldier for the government to support.

In George Griggs's *History of Mesilla Valley*, the Kid is credited with killing twenty-seven men—his first was a miner who ran off with the Kid's fifteen-year-old sister. The Kid follows the couple, and he tells the miner to marry the girl, but the miner couldn't do it as he was already married. Billy buys a six-shooter and kills the miner.

Colonel Maurice G. Fulton discovered four chapters of a personal narrative in the incomplete files of the Las Vegas *Optic* for 1882. On a visit to Billy's camp the narrator learned from the outlaw that his first victim was a Chinaman whose throat he cut from "ear to ear" for revealing that he had bought a keg of butter from him. Billy had sold his employer's butter and pocketed the money. The four stray chapters are available in *Folk-Say: A Regional Miscellany,* edited by B. A. Botkin, and issued by the University of New Mexico Press in 1930. This account gives Billy's birthplace as the county Limerick, Ireland.

FIGHTING AND FUN

With the Kid's career safely launched with whichever version you prefer, we turn to some of his early experiences. J. E. Sligh, a partner of Judge Ira A. Leonard in an assay office in

White Oaks in 1880, in an article in the *Overland Monthly,* July, 1908, tells a very thrilling story of one of the Kid's encounters with the Apaches. A rancher named Irvington leaves his wife and four children at home (near Fort Bayard) to go to the mountains, some five miles away, for a load of timber. Four renegade Apaches watch his departure and then surprise Mrs. Irvington and the children. One Apache guards the door; one the window; one seizes Mrs. Irvington; and one the oldest child, a "well-grown" girl of ten. Mrs. Irvington puts up a valiant fight but is knocked senseless. The three younger children hide under the bed. Just as Mrs. Irvington's captor is about to place her on the bed, the Kid makes a dramatic appearance, kills three of the Apaches and drives the other off. The author states "probably no other man on earth would have acted just as he did and accomplished what he did."

Kyle Crichton reports, in *Law and Order, Ltd.,* a visit to Albuquerque made by Elfego Baca and the Kid. Elfego and Billy ride from Socorro to Isleta, stable their horses with the Indians at the pueblo, and walk the thirteen miles into Albuquerque. Horses are not safe in Albuquerque, and rather than take a chance with the thieves the boys (Billy, seventeen and Elfego, sixteen) make the long walk in their high-heeled cowboy boots. On arriving in the "metropolis" they rest near a telegraph pole on First Street and almost immediately learn about "justice."

A policeman and a friend are talking as a man approaches. The man gets about ten steps past the policeman when the policeman hails him. As the man turns, the policeman shoots him down as the policeman's friend fires in the air. The friend places his smoking gun in the dead man's hand and takes the dead man's gun and places it in his own holster. Of course, the policeman is in the clear—self defense, and as he modestly admits, "I got the draw on him."

Elfego and the Kid visit the Martinez Bar in Old Town. (The Kid could have endeared himself to all at that famous old bar by playing the piano—"it was marvelous playing that Billy the Kid did"—but he was not in the mood.) The Kid has a short stubby revolver, and to the consternation of the customers he suddenly fires three shots into the rafters. The tough bouncer decides the Kid fired the shots since he is the calmest person in the bar; he searches Billy, but does not find the gun. A little later the Kid repeats the three shots into the rafters; he is searched again, and again the bouncer fails to locate the gun. The bouncer decides to throw the boys out, anyway, but the customers interfere. They finally leave and Billy reveals the location of the gun to Elfego—it is on top of his head adequately protected by his big "John B."

I want to point out that while the Kid was once seventeen and Elfego was once sixteen, it was not at the same time. According to author Crichton, Elfego was one year old in 1865, and that places the year of his birth as 1864. According to Garrett, the Kid was born in November, 1859, so Elfego was about five years younger than Billy.

"Billy the Kid's Lost Years" is the title of an article written for *The Texas Monthly,* September, 1929, by my friend Ramon Adams of Dallas. It is based on an interview with "Cyclone" Denton, old-time cowhand and frontiersman and later a two-gun man with Buffalo Bill's Wild West Show. "Cyclone" told Ramon that he worked with the Kid on the Gila Ranch in Arizona—the Kid was about sixteen at the time and Cyclone was nineteen. Cyclone said that the Kid was a good roper, a good rider, and a top hand. Billy was already a two-gun man, and he taught Cyclone how to use two guns—a skill that Cyclone utilized later in his act for Buffalo Bill's Show.

The Kid had an eye for a horse, and so did Cyclone, who owned a fine horse named Topsy. The Kid tried to trade Cyclone out of Topsy and, being unsuccessful, asked permission to ride him. Cyclone finally agreed, but on the condition that the Kid not use spurs, a quirt, or stiff bits. Topsy gave the Kid quite a ride—the Kid got a bloody nose, lost his hat, and finally pulled leather. Neither the Kid nor any other member of the crew ever asked to ride Topsy after that.

Cyclone remembered the Kid as smiling when he wasn't pleased and said that "a man who smiles that-a-way is dangerous." The Kid made a lot of friends on the Ranch, and Cyclone was his "buddy." Cyclone stated that even if the Kid did graze in the wrong pasture he liked him.

THE KID AND JESSE JAMES

Dr. Hoyt, the first practicing physician in the Texas Panhandle, in his fine book, *A Frontier Doctor,* tells about beating the Kid in a footrace at Tascosa. In the chapter "I Become a Bartender and Eat with Jesse James," he tells about the meeting between the Kid and James, who was traveling under his alias of "Mr. Howard." The two outlaws consider a merger, but Billy backs down. Homer Croy, in *Jesse James Was My Neighbor,* says it was the other way around—Jesse would have no part of the Kid.

John J. Collison in *Bill Jones of Paradise Valley, Oklahoma,* has a greatly different story to relate. Bill Jones goes to work for Dave Pool at his ranch in Colorado. Pool is a Missouri native and an old Quantrill raider. A rather good-looking young man, "more like a tenderfoot than a cowboy," rides up to the ranch looking for work. Though it is toward spring, Pool tells the young stranger that it is too early to put him to work but that there might be a job for him in two or three weeks. The young stranger sticks around taking many long rides to learn the range (or so he reports). One morning the stranger disappears and so does a considerable bunch of horses and some cattle. The same day, six well-armed riders arrive, and Jones learns that they are the real owners of the ranch. One of the men introduces the group to Jones—Frank James, Jesse James, Cole Younger, Bill Gregg, [and] Ike and George Berry. Reinforced with some cowboys, the gang takes the trail of the young stranger (and the cattle and horses). They meet some cowboys and learn that the rustler is no other than Billy the Kid. Under the leadership of Frank James, they press the pursuit and finally catch up with the Kid and his gang of nine. They kill eight of the Kid's men—only the Kid and one other escape under cover of night. The Kid does not last long after this fight as he is shot down by Pat Garrett. The Kid is twenty-three at the time he is killed and has twenty-three killings to his credit.

CAPTAIN TOM AND THE KID

The Young Pioneer—When Captain Tom Was a Boy quotes in full a letter from the Chief of Chaplains, War Department and includes a publisher's preface—both lending an air of authenticity that is undeserved. Captain Thomas Marion Hamilton's story about his life on the frontier is worthless as history but is a good example of the kind of "tall tale" spun for the grandchildren of a "participant." Almost half of the book is devoted to stories about Billy the Kid.

Captain Tom, at fourteen, is a cowboy on the McDermott ranch in New Mexico. The sheriff's posse traps the Kid in the Salinas cave. The Kid makes a deal with the deputy in charge of the posse when it comes under his guns in an open place near the mouth of the cave. The Kid orders Captain Tom to come to him, and he places his horse, Black Bess, in Captain Tom's charge since he has no horse feed in the cave. The posse begins the agreed withdrawal, but Sheriff Pat Garrett arrives and vetoes the arrangement. The posse settles down to starve the Kid out. A few days later Captain Tom wounds a mountain lion and trails it to another entrance to the cave. This entrance to the cave is unknown to the posse, and the Kid escapes through it just in the nick of time as the posse closes in on him. The grateful Billy presents his horse, Black Bess, to Captain Tom; the Kid's sweetheart, Maria Monette, is rescued from a gang of drunken Apaches by Captain Tom. She recognizes Black Bess and thereby Captain Tom. She is carrying the payroll from the bank in Santa Fe to the ranch when attacked by the Apaches.

The Kid is living in Arizona, under the name of Williams, and is going straight when he is arrested by mistake for killing a yearling that does not belong to him. It is a case of mistaken identity, but just as the Kid is cleared, Pat Garrett walks into the Tombstone courtroom. Pat sticks a gun into the Kid's back, but the Kid sidesteps and ducks and Pat's shot misses him. The Kid knocks Pat down with a blow to the jaw, but in the fight that follows the Kid is finally overpowered and captured. Maria Monette comes to Tombstone and helps the Kid escape to Mexico.

Later, the Kid warns Judge Fountain not to take his "last buckboard ride." The Judge ignores the warning, and both he and his young son are shot down by the Tate gang of cow thieves. Their bodies are buried in the White Sands. The foul deed is witnessed by the Kid and he becomes "The Mounted Ghost of Crawling White Sands" until the last member of the Tate gang is wiped out by his flaming guns. The Kid rides a white horse (with enormous rag boots tied to his feet), wears a white robe and lives at an Indian oasis in the White Sands until the last Tate is killed. (Note: Colonel Fountain and his son disappeared in 1896.)

Captain Tom becomes a mine owner in Mexico and the Kid visits him on several occasions when it gets too hot for him north of the border. During one of these visits the Kid helps Captain Tom clean up the Poe gang. This gang is trying to drive Captain Tom out of Mexico to gain possession of his mine.

Pat Garrett knows that the Kid visits Maria Monette occasionally. Pat goes to Maria and leads her to believe that if the Kid will surrender that he can persuade the judge and prosecuting attorney to let the Kid off with a light sentence of two or three years. Maria believes that Pat is sincere and arranges for the Kid to meet Pat at her ranch. The Kid arrives and is shot down by Pat who had concealed himself in Maria's garden. The furious girl tries to kill Pat but he disarms her. Captain Tom doesn't think much of Pat.

THE KILLING OF CARLYLE

Fred Sutton, peace officer as a young man, and Oklahoma oil man and banker in later years (and already mentioned), claims that Carlyle did not dive out of a window at the Greathouse ranch. Carlyle walked out the door, and Sutton knew, because he walked out with him. Sutton states that he accompanied Jimmy Carlyle on the fatal visit to the Greathouse ranch house and that the two of them were three-fourths the way back to the posse when the Kid's gang sent an avalanche of lead at them killing Carlyle, Sheriff William Bradley (Brady?) and George Hindman. Somehow, Sutton is not named as a posse member in any other account. In *The Trail Drivers of Texas,* Sutton offers no explanation for his own miraculous escape, but perhaps his story in the *Saturday Evening Post,* April, 10, 1926, provides a clue. In the Post article, Mr. Sutton tells how he saved Billy the Kid's life at a dance in Hays City. A greedy man is about to shoot the Kid in the back when Mr. Sutton knocks his gun up and shouts to warn the Kid. A few days later the Kid sends word that he will not forget that Sutton saved his life. In his book, *Hands up!,* the dance and the saving of the Kid's life seem to have occurred at Tascosa. Take your choice.

THE JOURNAL OF A SISTER OF CHARITY

The dates in the journal of a Sister of Charity, *At the End of the Santa Fe Trail* (Columbus, Ohio, 1932), must be considered to be editorial, since they do not check with established facts. According to the journal, Sister Blandina nurses a member of the Kid's gang and saves the lives of Trinidad's doctors by "getting the grateful Kid to grant her a favor." The favor is, of course, the sparing of the lives of the doctors. This incident occurs in September, 1876, and despite the care given the wounded bandit, he dies December 2, 1876.

Sister Blandina encounters the Kid again on June 9, 1878. She is en route by stage from Trinidad to Santa Fe when the Kid stops the stage, probably to rob it. He recognizes Sister Blandina and rides away.

In January, 1881, her journal entry states that the Kid is using his gun freely, and that Governor Wallace's interviews with him have had no effect.

The entry for July 23, 1881, reveals that the Kid is "playing high pranks" and that there are big rewards offered for his capture.

On May 16, 1882, Sister Blandina goes to see the Kid in jail—he is chained hand and foot. He asks nothing for himself but entreats the good Sister to do what she can for Kelly, a fellow prisoner and first offender.

The entry for September 8, 1882, records the killing of "poor, poor Billy the Kid" by Sheriff Pat Garrett.

Later Harry C. Gibbs wrote a one-act play, *Chico,* around the first Billy the Kid incident recorded in Sister Blandina's journal.

MOB SCENE AT LAS VEGAS

"I was there" seems to be a favorite term in many personal narratives, particularly as concerning major events. At least three "eye-witness" accounts of the mob scene at Las Vegas are available in addition to Pat Garrett's matter-of-fact statement in his *The Authentic Life of Billy the Kid.* In fact, the last part of Pat's book can easily be classed as a personal narrative as it is a rather matter-of-fact account of a manhunt and is set down in Pat's plain language. If Ash Upson "wrote" the entire book, it seems certain that the description of events, after Pat personally became a participant, is by Pat and that he allowed Ash few liberties in changing his words in the process of writing down the story as he related it.

Albert Hyde's account was printed in the *Century Magazine*, March, 1902. Hyde, a young Tennesseean, was in Las Vegas when Pat Garrett arrived there with his prisoners after the surrender at Stinking Springs. His article, though written sometime later, is an eyewitness account of Pat's coolness in the face of danger when the mob demanded his prisoners. The Mexican population at Las Vegas was bitter towards Dave Rudabaugh, who had killed the jailer there in making good his escape from the jail a few months before. The mob seemed much more intent on getting its hands on Rudabaugh than it was in taking the Kid. From a vantage point, on top a nearby box car, Hyde observes the action of the officers and the prisoners. He states that Rudabaugh smoked a cigar and seemed uninterested while the Kid became very excited and asked Pat to return his guns should the mob attack. Garrett gives a very different version of the reactions of the prisoners and states that he promised the prisoners he would arm them should there be a fight with the mob.

Hyde is high in his praise of Pat's conduct on this occasion.

Jim McIntire, in *Early Days in Texas: A Trip to Hell and Heaven* (Kansas City, 1902), states that he was City Marshal at Las Vegas when Sheriff Pat Garrett, Jim East, and two other deputies brought in the Kid, Dave Rudabaugh, Tom Pickett, Bill Wilson and Tom Fowler. McIntire noted the gathering of the mob and fearing that it would try to take Rudabaugh by force, he went into town and gathered up a few guns with which to arm the prisoner in the case of violence. However, Sheriff Pat Garrett stood firm and as the train started with a jerk, the Kid opened a window and let out a war whoop which scattered the Mexicans in all directions. The Kid is called the "notorious Mexican outlaw" by McIntire.

Former Governor Miguel Antonio Otero in his first book, *My Life on the Frontier—1864–1882,* tells the story of the mob's attempt to prevent Pat taking Rudabaugh on to Santa Fe. The Governor "quotes" Pat's speech to the mob, made from the car of the train that was to take the prisoners to Santa Fe. The Governor's father, one of the town's most substantial citizens, then climbs to the car platform and, after shaking hands with Pat, urges the mob to disband. He assures the people of Las Vegas that Pat is a man of his word and that the prisoners will be delivered to the proper authorities at Santa Fe. The mob disbands.

The Governor and his brother ride the train from Las Vegas to Santa Fe with Pat and his prisoners. They talk with the Kid and Rudabaugh, an old acquaintance. They visit the Kid many times at the jail at Santa Fe. The Governor likes the Kid and his appraisal of the Kid's character is supported by Mrs. Jaramillo (of Fort Sumner) and Don Martin Chaves. The Governor concludes that the Kid was "a man more sinned against than sinning."

1881—THE FINAL SCENES

Tex Moore "was there" when the Kid escaped at Lincoln. In his book, *The West,* this is the story: "Tex," his "pard" Steve, and

Billy Kind are eating dinner at the Wortley Hotel in Lincoln, hear the shot that kills Bell, and see the Kid kill Bob Ollinger. The Kid waves good-bye and shouts, "So long boys," to them as he rides out of Lincoln.

Frederick William Grey wrote the story of his American experiences some years after returning to England. His book, *Seeking Fortune in America* (London, 1912), gives Kip McKinney's version of the killing of the Kid. Grey works with Kipp Kinney (Kip McKinney) on a mining venture in the Southwest, and from him hears the story of the killing of the Kid told in this book. Grey compares the Kid with Ben Thompson and gives Ben all the best of it. He states that the Kid never fought fair, being a half-breed Indian. As he recalls the story told him by Kipp, Pat Garrett learns that the Kid will visit his Mexican sweetheart. Pat and Kipp arrive at her home before the Kid, and they tie up and gag the girl. Pat hides behind a sofa while Kipp stands guard outside. As the Kid enters his girl's house he shows clearly in the open door for a moment, and Pat shoots him down. Grey comments, "This was not showing much sporting spirit."

John Lord, mentioned earlier, tells it this way: The Kid is in love with a Mexican girl, whose father works for Pete Maxwell at Fort Sumner. Maxwell's foreman, fine young Mexican, loves the same girl. The girl and her mother favor the Kid but the girl's father prefers the ranch foreman. The father knows when the Kid is due to call because the women do an especially good job of cleaning the house. Through the foreman, the father gets word to the Sheriff.

Lord arrives at Maxwell's to buy some cattle and Maxwell assigns his own bedroom to Lord. Deputy Pat Garrett, having received word that the Kid is due, arrives disguised as a Mexican. Lord and Pat go to bed in Maxwell's bed—Pat is fully clad and occupies the back half of the bed which is quite aways from the wall. They hear the Kid coming and Pat slides off the bed and squats between the bed and the wall, with cocked gun in hand. Billy steps in the room and Pat raises up and shoots right over Lord. Billy falls dead with a bullet through his heart. Billy is twenty-four and had killed twenty-four men at the time of his death.

I want to recommend that you read Tom Blevins's tale in the Late Lloyd Lewis's *It Takes All Kinds* (New York, 1947). This is probably the wildest of all the old-timer tales of the Kid.

I have purposely omitted the personal narratives of Charley Siringo (*A Texas Cowboy*), George Coe (*Frontier Fighter*), John W. Poe (*The True Story of the Death of Billy the Kid*) as being entirely too factual and too well known to fit into the theme of this presentation. I hope the material chosen was partially new, at least to most of you, and that you are tantalized enough by this sample to take the trail of the Kid in many other personal narratives. And perhaps you can then help me understand why good men and true vie for the honor of "having known" such killers as Billy the Kid.

O. HENRY
"THE CABALLERO'S WAY"

William Sydney Porter, who worked under the pseudonym O. Henry, wrote about the locales, people, and stories with which he was familiar. And he was very familiar with the West of the 1880s and 1890s. He'd located to Texas in 1882, working at assorted jobs, including draftsman, bank teller, and journalist.

O. Henry's famous story "The Caballero's Way" introduces a character inspired by Billy the Kid, a shootist the author renames the Cisco Kid. O. Henry was no doubt affected by early stage productions about Billy the Kid and stories he had heard about Billy the Kid and Joaquin Muiretta. Few articles, essays, or stories have been as important to creating Billy the Kid's mythology as "The Caballero's Way." The central character, the Cisco Kid, has further evolved into one of the most enduring figure in modern pop culture, with inclusions in comic books, television series, and more than twenty-five movies.

SELECTED STORIES OF O. HENRY

With an Introduction and Notes

By Victoria Blake
1907

The Cisco Kid had killed six men in more or less fair scrimmages, had murdered twice as many (mostly Mexicans), and had winged a larger number whom he modestly forbore to count. Therefore a woman loved him.

The Kid was twenty-five, looked twenty; and a careful insurance company would have estimated the probable time of his demise at, say, twenty-six. His habitat was anywhere between the Frio and the Rio Grande. He killed for the love of it— because he was quick-tempered—to avoid arrest—for his own amusement—any reason that came to his mind would suffice. He had escaped capture because he could shoot five-sixths of a second sooner than any sheriff or ranger in the service, and because he rode a speckled roan horse that knew every cowpath in the mesquite and pear thickets from San Antonio to Matamoras.

Tonia Perez, the girl who loved the Cisco Kid, was half Carmen, half Madonna, and the rest—oh, yes, a woman who is half Carmen and half Madonna can always be something more—the rest, let us say, was humming-bird. She lived in a grass-roofed *jacal* [hut] near a little Mexican settlement at the Lone Wolf Crossing of the Frio. With her lived a father or grandfather, a lineal Aztec, somewhat less than a thousand years old, who herded a hundred goats and lived in a continuous drunken dream of drinking *mescal*. Back of the *jacal* a tremendous forest of bristling pear, twenty feet high at its worst, crowded almost to its door. It was along the bewildering maze of this spinous thicket that the speckled roan would bring the Kid to see his girl. And once, clinging like a lizard to the ridgepole, high up under the peaked grass roof, he had heard Tonia, with her Madonna face and Carmen beauty and humming-bird soul, parley with the sheriff's posse, denying knowledge of her man in her soft *mélange* of Spanish and English.

One day the adjutant-general of the State, who is *ex-officio*, commander of the ranger forces, wrote some sarcastic lines to Captain Duval of Company X, stationed at Laredo, relative to the serene and undisturbed existence led by murderers and desperadoes in the said captain's territory.

The captain turned the colour of brick dust under his tan, and forwarded the letter, after adding a few comments, per ranger Private Bill Adamson, to ranger Lieutenant Sandridge, camped at a water hole on the Nueces with a squad of five men in preservation of law and order.

Lieutenant Sandridge turned a beautiful *couleur de rose* through his ordinary strawberry complexion, tucked the letter in his hip pocket, and chewed off the ends of his gamboge moustache.

The next morning he saddled his horse and rode alone to the Mexican settlement at the Lone Wolf Crossing of the Frio, twenty miles away.

Six feet two, blond as a Viking, quiet as a deacon, dangerous as a machine gun, Sandridge moved among the *Jacales*, patiently seeking news of the Cisco Kid.

Far more than the law, the Mexicans dreaded the cold and certain vengeance of the lone rider that the ranger sought. It had been one of the Kid's pastimes to shoot Mexicans "to see them kick": if he demanded from them moribund Terpsichorean feats, simply that he might be entertained, what terrible and extreme penalties would be certain to follow should they anger him! One and all they lounged with upturned palms and shrugging shoulders, filling the air with "*quien sabes*" and denials of the Kid's acquaintance.

But there was a man named Fink who kept a store at the Crossing—a man of many nationalities, tongues, interests, and ways of thinking.

"No use to ask them Mexicans," he said to Sandridge. "They're afraid to tell. This *hombre* they call the Kid—Goodall is his name, ain't it?—he's been in my store once or twice. I have an idea you might run across him at—but I guess I don't keer to say, myself. I'm two seconds later in pulling a gun than I used to be, and the difference is worth thinking about. But this Kid's got a half-Mexican girl at the Crossing that he comes to see. She lives in that *jacal* a hundred yards down the arroyo at the edge of the pear. Maybe she—no, I don't suppose she would, but that *jacal* would be a good place to watch, anyway."

Sandridge rode down to the *jacal* of Perez. The sun was low, and the broad shade of the great pear thicket already covered the grass-thatched hut. The goats were enclosed for the night in a brush corral near by. A few kids walked the top of it, nibbling the chaparral leaves. The old Mexican lay upon a blanket on the grass, already in a stupor from his mescal, and dreaming, perhaps, of the nights when he and Pizarro touched glasses to their New World fortunes—so old his wrinkled face seemed to proclaim him to be. And in the door of the *jacal* stood Tonia. And Lieutenant Sandridge sat in his saddle staring at her like a gannet agape at a sailorman.

The Cisco Kid was a vain person, as all eminent and successful assassins are, and his bosom would have been ruffled had he known that at a simple exchange of glances two persons, in whose minds he had been looming large, suddenly abandoned (at least for the time) all thought of him.

Never before had Tonia seen such a man as this. He seemed to be made of sunshine and blood-red tissue and clear weather. He seemed to illuminate the shadow of the pear when he smiled, as though the sun were rising again. The men she had known had been small and dark. Even the Kid, in spite of his achievements, was a stripling no larger than herself, with black, straight hair and a cold, marble face that chilled the noonday.

As for Tonia, though she sends description to the poorhouse, let her make a millionaire of your fancy. Her blue-black hair, smoothly divided in the middle and bound close to her head, and her large eyes full of the Latin melancholy, gave her the Madonna touch. Her motions and air spoke of the concealed fire and the desire to charm that she had inherited from the *gitanas* of the Basque province. As for the humming-bird part of her, that dwelt in her heart; you could not perceive it unless her bright red skirt and dark blue blouse gave you a symbolic hint of the vagarious bird.

The newly lighted sun-god asked for a drink of water. Tonia brought it from the red jar hanging under the brush shelter. Sandridge considered it necessary to dismount so as to lessen the trouble of her ministrations.

I play no spy; nor do I assume to master the thoughts of any human heart; but I assert, by the chronicler's right, that before a quarter of an hour had sped, Sandridge was teaching her how to plait a six-strand rawhide stake-rope, and Tonia had explained to him that were it not for her little English book that the peripatetic padre had given her and the little crippled *chivo* [billy goat], that she fed from a bottle, she would be very, very lonely indeed.

Which leads to a suspicion that the Kid's fences needed repairing, and that the adjutant-general's sarcasm had fallen upon unproductive soil.

In his camp by the water hole Lieutenant Sandridge announced and reiterated his intention of either causing the Cisco Kid to nibble the black loam of the Frio country prairies or of haling him before a judge and jury. That sounded business-like. Twice a week he rode over to the Lone Wolf Crossing of the Frio, and directed Tonia's slim, slightly lemon-tinted fingers among the intricacies of the slowly growing lariata [braided rope used like a lasso]. A six-strand plait is hard to learn and easy to teach.

The ranger knew that he might find the Kid there at any visit. He kept his armament ready, and had a frequent eye for the pear thicket at the rear of the *jacal*. Thus he might bring down the kite and the humming-bird with one stone.

While the sunny-haired ornithologist was pursuing his studies the Cisco Kid was also attending to his professional duties. He moodily shot up a saloon in a small cow village on Quintana Creek, killed the town marshal (plugging him neatly in the centre of his tin badge), and then rode away, morose and unsatisfied. No true artist is uplifted by shooting an aged man carrying an old-style .38 bulldog.

On his way the Kid suddenly experienced the yearning that all men feel when wrong-doing loses its keen edge of delight.

He yearned for the woman he loved to reassure him that she was his in spite of it. He wanted her to call his bloodthirstiness bravery and his cruelty devotion. He wanted Tonia to bring him water from the red jar under the brush shelter, and tell him how the *chivo* was thriving on the bottle.

The Kid turned the speckled roan's head up the ten-mile pear flat that stretches along the Arroyo Hondo until it ends at the Lone Wolf Crossing of the Frio. The roan whickered; for he had a sense of locality and direction equal to that of a belt-line street-car horse; and he knew he would soon be nibbling the rich mesquite grass at the end of a forty-foot stake-rope while Ulysses rested his head in Circe's straw-footed hut.

More weird and lonesome than the journey of an Amazonian explorer is the ride of one through a Texas pear flat. With dismal monotony and startling variety the uncanny and multiform shapes of the cacti lift their twisted trunks, and fat, bristly hands to encumber the way. The demon plant, appearing to live without soil or rain, seems to taunt the parched traveler with its lush grey greenness. It warps itself a thousand times about what look to be open and inviting paths, only to lure the rider into blind and impassable spine-defended "bottoms of the bag," leaving him to retreat, if he can, with the points of the compass whirling in his head.

To be lost in the pear is to die almost the death of the thief on the cross, pierced by nails and with grotesque shapes of all the fiends hovering about.

But it was not so with the Kid and his mount. Winding, twisting, circling, tracing the most fantastic and bewildering trail ever picked out, the good roan lessened the distance to the Lone Wolf Crossing with every coil and turn that he made.

While they fared the Kid sang. He knew but one tune and sang it, as he knew but one code and lived it, and but one girl and loved her. He was a single-minded man of conventional ideas. He had a voice like a coyote with bronchitis, but whenever he chose to sing his song he sang it. It was a conventional song of the camps and trail, running at its beginning as near as may be to these words:

> Don't you monkey with my Lulu girl
> Or I'll tell you what I'll do—

And so on. The roan was inured to it, and did not mind.

But even the poorest singer will, after a certain time, gain his own consent to refrain from contributing to the world's noises. So the Kid, by the time he was within a mile or two of Tonia's *jacal,* had reluctantly allowed his song to die away—not because his vocal performance had become less charming to his own ears, but because his laryngeal muscles were aweary.

As though he were in a circus ring the speckled roan wheeled and danced through the labyrinth of pear until at length his rider knew by certain landmarks that the Lone Wolf Crossing was close at hand. Then, where the pear was thinner, he caught sight of the grass roof of the *jacal* and the hackberry tree on the edge of the arroyo. A few yards farther the Kid stopped the roan and gazed intently through the prickly openings. Then he dismounted, dropped the roan's reins, and proceeded on foot, stooping and silent, like an Indian. The roan, knowing his part, stood still, making no sound.

The Kid crept noiselessly to the very edge of the pear thicket and reconnoitered between the leaves of a clump of cactus.

Ten yards from his hiding-place, in the shade of the *jacal*, sat his Tonia calmly plaiting a rawhide lariat. So far she might surely escape condemnation; women have been known, from time to time, to engage in more mischievous occupations. But if all must be told, there is to be added that her head reposed against the broad and comfortable chest of a tall red-and-yellow man, and that his arm was about her, guiding her nimble small fingers that required so many lessons at the intricate six-strand plait.

Sandridge glanced quickly at the dark mass of pear when he heard a slight squeaking sound that was not altogether unfamiliar. A gun-scabbard will make that sound when one grasps the handle of a six-shooter suddenly. But the sound was not repeated; and Tonia's fingers needed close attention.

And then, in the shadow of death, they began to talk to their love; and in the still July afternoon every word they uttered reached the ears of the Kid.

"Remember, then," said Tonia, "you must not come again until I send for you. Soon he will be here. A *vaquero* at the *tienda* said to-day he saw him on the Guadalupe three days ago. When he is that near he always comes. If he comes and finds you here he will kill you. So, for my sake, you must come no more until I send you the word."

"All right," said the ranger. "And then what?"

"And then," said the girl, "you must bring your men here and kill him. If not, he will kill you."

"He ain't a man to surrender, that's sure," said Sandridge. "It's kill or be killed for the officer that goes up against Mr. Cisco Kid."

"He must die," said the girl. "Otherwise there will not be

any peace in the world for thee and me. He has killed many. Let him so die. Bring your men, and give him no chance to escape."

"You used to think right much of him," said Sandridge.

Tonia dropped the lariat, twisted herself around, and curved a lemon-tinted arm over the ranger's shoulder.

"But then," she murmured in liquid Spanish, "I had not beheld thee, thou great, red mountain of a man! And thou art kind and good, as well as strong. Could one choose him, knowing thee? Let him die; for then I will not be filled with fear by day and night lest he hurt thee or me."

"How can I know when he comes?" asked Sandridge.

"When he comes," said Tonia, "he remains two days, sometimes three. Gregorio, the small son of old Luisa, the *lavandera,* has a swift pony. I will write a letter to thee and send it by him, saying how it will be best to come upon him. By Gregorio will the letter come. And bring many men with thee, and have much care, oh, dear red one, for the rattlesnake is not quicker to strike than is '*El Chivato,*' as they call him, to send a ball from his *pistola.*"

"The Kid's handy with his gun, sure enough," admitted Sandridge, "but when I come for him I shall come alone. I'll get him by myself or not at all. The Cap wrote one or two things to me that make me want to do the trick without any help. You let me know when Mr. Kid arrives, and I'll do the rest."

"I will send you the message by the boy Gregorio," said the girl. "I knew you were braver than that small slayer of men who never smiles. How could I ever have thought I cared for him?"

It was time for the ranger to ride back to his camp on the water hole. Before he mounted his horse he raised the slight form of Tonia with one arm high from the earth for a parting salute. The drowsy stillness of the torpid summer air still lay thick upon the dreaming afternoon. The smoke from the fire in the *jacal,* where the *frijoles* blubbered in the iron pot, rose straight as a plumb-line above the clay-daubed chimney. No sound or movement disturbed the serenity of the dense pear thicket ten yards away.

When the form of Sandridge had disappeared, loping his big dun down the steep banks of the Frio crossing, the Kid crept back to his own horse, mounted him, and rode back along the tortuous trail he had come.

But not far. He stopped and waited in the silent depths of the pear until half an hour had passed. And then Tonia heard the high, untrue notes of his unmusical singing coming nearer and nearer; and she ran to the edge of the pear to meet him.

The Kid seldom smiled; but he smiled and waved his hat when he saw her. He dismounted, and his girl sprang into his arms. The Kid looked at her fondly. His thick, black hair clung to his head like a wrinkled mat. The meeting brought a slight ripple of some undercurrent of feeling to his smooth, dark face that was usually as motionless as a clay mask.

"How's my girl?" he asked, holding her close.

"Sick of waiting so long for you, dear one," she answered. "My eyes are dim with always gazing into that devil's pincushion through which you come. And I can see into it such a little way, too. But you are here, beloved one, and I will not scold. *Que mal muchacho!* not to come to see you *alma* more often. Go in and rest, and let me water your horse and stake him with the long rope. There is cool water in the jar for you."

The Kid kissed her affectionately.

"Not if the court knows itself do I let a lady stake my horse for me," said he. "But if you'll run in, *chica,* and throw a pot of coffee together while I attend to the *caballo,* I'll be a good deal obliged."

Besides his marksmanship the Kid had another attribute for which he admired himself greatly. He was *muy caballero,* as the Mexicans express it, where the ladies were concerned. For them he had always gentle words and consideration. He could not have spoken a harsh word to a woman. He might ruthlessly slay their husbands and brothers, but he could not have laid the weight of a finger in anger upon a woman. Wherefore many of that interesting division of humanity who had come under the spell of his politeness declared their disbelief in the stories circulated about Mr. Kid. One shouldn't believe everything one heard, they said. When confronted by the indignant men folk with proof of the *caballero's* deeds of infamy, they said maybe he had been driven to it, and that he knew how to treat a lady, anyhow.

Considering this extremely courteous idiosyncrasy of the Kid and the pride that he took in it, one can perceive that the solution of the problem that was presented to him by what he saw and heard from his hiding-place in the pear that afternoon (at least as to one of the actors) must have been obscured by difficulties. And yet one could not think of the Kid overlooking little matters of that kind.

At the end of the short twilight they gathered around a supper of *frijoles,* goat steaks, canned peaches, and coffee, by the light of a lantern in the *jacal.* Afterward, the ancestor, his flock corralled, smoked a cigarette and became a mummy in a grey blanket. Tonia washed the few dishes while the Kid dried them with the flour-sacking towel. Her eyes shone; she chatted volubly of the inconsequent happenings of her small world since the Kid's last visit; it was as all his other home-comings had been.

Then outside Tonia swung in a grass hammock with her guitar and sang sad *canciones de amor.*

"Do you love me just the same, old girl?" asked the Kid, hunting for his cigarette papers.

"Always the same, little one," said Tonia, her dark eyes lingering upon him.

"I must go over to Fink's," said the Kid, rising, "for some tobacco. I thought I had another sack in my coat. I'll be back in a quarter of an hour."

"Hasten," said Tonia, "and tell me—how long shall I call you my own this time? Will you be gone again to-morrow, leaving me to grieve, or will you be longer with your Tonia?"

"Oh, I might stay two or three days this trip," said the Kid, yawning. "I've been on the dodge for a month, and I'd like to rest up."

He was gone half an hour for his tobacco. When he returned Tonia was still lying in the hammock.

"It's funny," said the Kid, "how I feel. I feel like there was somebody lying behind every bush and tree waiting to shoot me. I never had mullygrubs like them before. Maybe it's one of them presumptions. I've got half a notion to light out in the morning before day. The Guadalupe country is burning up about that old Dutchman I plugged down there."

"You are not afraid—no one could make my brave little one fear."

"Well, I haven't been usually regarded as a jack-rabbit when it comes to scrapping; but I don't want a posse smoking me out when I'm in your *jacal.* Somebody might get hurt that oughtn't to."

"Remain with your Tonia; no one will find you here."

The Kid looked keenly into the shadows up and down the arroyo and toward the dim lights of the Mexican village.

"I'll see how it looks later on," was his decision.

At midnight a horseman rode into the rangers' camp, blazing his way by noisy "halloes" to indicate a pacific mission. Sandridge and one or two others turned out to investigate the row. The rider announced himself to be Domingo Sales, from the Lone Wolf Crossing. He bore a letter for Señor Sandridge. Old Luisa, the *lavendera,* had persuaded him to bring it, he said, her son Gregorio being too ill of a fever to ride.

Sandridge lighted the camp lantern and read the letter. These were its words:

DEAR ONE: He has come. Hardly had you ridden away when he came out of the pear. When he first talked he said he would stay three days or more. Then as it grew later he was like a wolf or a fox, and walked about without rest, looking and listening. Soon he said he must leave before daylight when it is dark and stillest. And then he seemed to suspect that I be not true to him. He looked at me so strange that I am frightened. I swear to him that I love him, his own Tonia. Last of all he said I must prove to him I am true. He thinks that even now men are waiting to kill him as he rides from my house. To escape he says he will dress in my clothes, my red skirt and the blue waist I wear and the brown mantilla over the head, and thus ride away. But before that he says that I must put on his clothes, his *pantalones* and *camisa* and hat, and ride away on his horse from the jacal as far as the big road beyond the crossing and back again. This before he goes, so he can tell if I am true and if men are hidden to shoot him. It is a terrible thing. An hour before daybreak this is to be. Come, my dear one, and kill this man and take me for your Tonia. Do not try to take hold of him alive, but kill him quickly. Knowing all, you should do that. You must come long before the time and hide yourself in the little shed near the *jacal* where the wagon and saddles are kept. It is dark in there. He will wear my red skirt and blue waist and brown mantilla. I send you a hundred kisses. Come surely and shoot quickly and straight.

THINE OWN TONIA.

Sandridge quickly explained to his men the official part of the missive. The rangers protested against his going alone.

"I'll get him easy enough," said the lieutenant. "The girl's got him trapped. And don't even think he'll get the drop on me."

Sandridge saddled his horse and rode to the Lone Wolf Crossing. He tied his big dun in a clump of brush on the arroyo, took his Winchester from its scabbard, and carefully approached the Perez *jacal*. There was only the half of a high moon drifted over by ragged, milk-white gulf clouds.

The wagon-shed was an excellent place for ambush; and the ranger got inside it safely. In the black shadow of the brush shelter in front of the *jacal* he could see a horse tied and hear him impatiently pawing the hard-trodden earth.

He waited almost an hour before two figures came out of the *jacal*. One, in man's clothes, quickly mounted the horse and galloped past the wagon-shed toward the crossing and village. And then the other figure, in skirt, waist, and mantilla over its head, stepped out into the faint moonlight, gazing after the rider. Sandridge thought he would take his chance then before Tonia rode back. He fancied she might not care to see it.

"Throw up your hands," he ordered loudly, stepping out of the wagon-shed with his Winchester at his shoulder.

There was a quick turn of the figure, but no movement to obey, so the ranger pumped in the bullets—one—two—three—and then twice more; for you never could be too sure of bringing down the Cisco Kid. There was no danger of missing at ten paces even in that half moonlight.

The old ancestor, asleep on his blanket, was awakened by the shots. Listening further, he heard a great cry from some man in mortal distress or anguish, and rose up grumbling at the disturbing ways of moderns.

The tall, red ghost of a man burst into the *jacal*, reaching one hand, shaking like a *tule* reed, for the lantern hanging on its nail. The other spread a letter on the table.

"Look at this letter, Perez," cried the man. "Who wrote it?"

"*Ah, Dios!* it is Señor Sandridge," mumbled the old man, approaching. "*Pues, señor,* that letter was written by '*El Chivato,*' as he is called—by the man of Tonia. They say he is a bad man; I do not know. While Tonia slept he wrote the letter and sent it by this old hand of mine to Domingo Sales to be brought to you. Is there anything wrong in the letter? I am very old; and I did not know. *Valgame Dios!* it is a very foolish world; and there is nothing in the house to drink—nothing to drink."

Just then all that Sandridge could think of to do was to go outside and throw himself face downward in the dust by the side of his humming-bird, of whom not a feather fluttered. He was not a *caballero* by instinct, and he could not understand the niceties of revenge.

A mile away the rider who had ridden past the wagon-shed struck up a harsh, untuneful song, the words of which began:

> Don't you monkey with my Lulu girl
> Or I'll tell you what I'll do—

N. HOWARD "JACK" THORP
BILLY ("THE KID") BONNEY

N. Howard "Jack" Thorp moved to the West to ranch and collect cowboy songs. His two collections, Songs of the Cowboys *(1908) and* Tales of the Chuck Wagon *(1926), are considered classics.*

Along the way, Thorp collected many a good Western story, including several about Billy the Kid. One of his interests was how legends are created, and here he gives special attention to the Kid, delving into Pat Garrett's motivations and examining, as many others have, the matter of how many men Billy the Kid actually killed. Thorp's count falls far short of the twenty-one of legend.

Here is a story found in Pardner of the Wind: Story of the Southwestern Cowboy.

FROM
PARDNER OF THE WIND
Story of the Southwestern Cowboy

By N. Howard (Jack) Thorp
In collaboration with Neil M. Clark
1941

———•◦•———

Bustin' down the canyon,
Horses on the run,
Posse just behind them,
'Twas June first, seventy-one.

Saddle guns in scabbards,
Pistols on saddle bow,
The boys were ridin' for their lives—
The Kid en Alias Joe.

I

Of all the New Mexico "bad men," William H. Bonney, known as Billy the Kid, is by far the most famous. Sixty years after his sordid death, native women still scare their children by telling them "Bilito" will come and get them if they don't behave. Armchair adventure hounds halfway around the world scare themselves under their reading lamps over lurid accounts of his alleged exploits. His career has even been put in the movies, and from now on he will probably be pictured in the public mind as two-gun Robert Taylor.

There seem to have been about as many contradictions in Billy's character as in that of "Bad Man" Moore—he was part good and part bad, like most of the rest of us. But the most curious thing about Billy is not what he actually was, in the flesh, but the steps by which his reputation grew so that he is now transformed into the kind of person the thrill-hungry public imagines him to be. He is not history any more, but legend, romanticized out of all likeness to the gun-totin', rambunctious, carefree cowboy kid that his friends and enemies knew, and he has become a sort of super-hero. It is hard, maybe impossible, to separate the truth about him from falsehood, the facts from the fiction. However, that is what I have tried to do, and in this chapter I aim to examine some of the evidence concerning a very curious phenomenon in the history of the West.

Actually, Billy the Kid was just a little, small-sized cow- and horse-thief who lived grubbily and missed legal hanging by only a few days. He killed, or took part in killing, several people; but his killings were more often on the order of safe butchery than stand-up-and-fight-it-out gun battles. He took part in a range war on the losing side. He died, not in a blaze of glory, but like a butchered yearling, shot down in the dead of night in his stocking feet, when he was armed with a butcher knife and, possibly, though not certainly, with a six-shooter. Yet for all that, romance does cling to his name. Half a dozen books about him have been written and published. The town of Lincoln, New Mexico, thrives on his memory. And many people regard him as a sort of super-Robin Hood of the range, a daredevil of matchless courage, haloed by smoke wreathing upward from fogging guns. He makes a fascinating study in the technique and psychology of literary and national hero creation. Many have told the "facts" about Bill. Few have agreed about them. The heavy shadow of the "hero" tradition has made unconscious liars of some; others have lied about him on purpose, loading the public with tall tales to satisfy the appetites of listeners greedy for shudders and blood.

I, of course, did not know Billy. He died too young. His bones had been mouldering in the dust of old Fort Sumner for nearly ten years when I first laid eyes on the sunny flats and mountain ranges beyond the Pecos where the bloody events in which he shared, took place. But I knew Lincoln County intimately, and I knew many of those who knew him, including Sheriff Pat Garrett, who fired the shot that killed him; George Coe, who rode and bunked with him for months when matters were at their worst; Charlie Siringo who, although he knew Billy only slightly, wrote a small and highly-colored book about him; and many more. To most of those who knew him, Billy was no hero. To some, he was a good friend and a likable companion. Others considered him no better than any other brand-blotting thief, and a coward besides. The truth seems to lie somewhere between these extremes, as it usually does in judging the characters of people. But it is the growth of the hero myth that I am particularly interested to examine, thinking it might shed light on the deification of certain other "heroes" in our modern world, such as Adolf of Berchtesgaden and John Dillinger.

The Kid's background was certainly colorful. The years that made his fame were spent on or near the Pecos River, which well deserves its other name, the River of Sin. The Pecos rises in the Sangre de Cristo Mountains at an elevation of ten thousand feet, and after cascading down rocky slopes wild with pine, aspen, and juniper, breaks out into the flat country near old Fort Sumner. Thence toward the south it threads the old cattle range of the Chisums, and on into Texas, finally entering the Rio Grande in a rocky gorge north and west of Del Rio, not far from Judge Roy Bean's town, Langtry. For several hundred miles the Pecos passes through a country almost destitute of trees, meagerly fed by five rivers from the west that have their origin in the Guadalupes, and by two from the east—Pintada Canyon, and Alamogordo Creek. The very name of the river came to stand for murder, for when the freebooters of the valley killed a man, they were said to have "Pecos'd" him, meaning, tied stones to his dead body and rolled it into the river. Three races, Indian, Spanish, and English, with a scattering of French and others, met, mixed, and fought in this valley. It is likely that the country that became Billy the Kid's playground, is richer than any other in the West in tales of lost mines, buried treasures, cattle wars, bloody violence, and mysterious happenings.

No one, for example, has ever explained the mystery of the three human skeletons found on the upper Pecos, together with their guns, saddles, and camp equipment, and a buckskin bag full of nuggets and placer gold. The guns were ancient cap-and-ball pistols, and two shots had been fired from one of the guns, one shot apiece from each of the others. Nor has anyone, presumably, ever found out where the bandits buried the gold they took when they robbed the stagecoach a few miles east of the Pecos River. The bandits, lost in a blind canyon, were overtaken promptly and killed near the river, but the stolen gold was not on them. Nor does anyone have an accurate record of the number of bloody battles that were fought at or near the site of the Pecos Pueblo, first between Plains and Pueblo Indians, and later between the Pueblos and the Spaniards.

A little to the west of the river stands the tragic Sierito Bernál, now called Starvation Peak, where a wagonload of emigrants fled when attacked by Indians. Besieged there constantly by the Indians, without food or water, all starved to death. This area, too, and the whole country from Las Vegas to Santa Fe, was the stronghold of *Vicente Silva y sus Quarenta Bandidos*—night riders who wore long white sheets with red daggers embroidered on the back, and who, when they rode into a town four abreast and a hundred strong, always left behind some victim of their vengeance, his corpse perhaps not being found for months.

Old Fort Sumner, on the east side of the Pecos, was founded in 1862, expressly to prevent bloodshed on the Bosque Redondo Indian Reserve, where thousands of bloodthirsty Apache and Navajo Indians had been placed. Two companies of cavalry had their barracks here.

In the town of Roswell, further down the river, Sheriff Charles Perry, in order to keep the peace, had to kill three men in one day, while at Eddy (now Carlsbad) certain hard characters murdered the sheriff in broad daylight.

Two miles south of Eddy was a collection of saloons and dance halls, populated by the riffraff and outcasts of Eddy, the place being known as Phoenix. One of the houses here was run by a man named Barfield, who "fell from under his hat" when shot from the outside through the window. Across the street was a place run by Ed Lyalls and his wife, Nellie, frequented by a gang who paid for their liquor with stolen cattle. I stopped at Lyalls' place once for a few minutes on the way back to my ranch on Black River, and while I was there, two strangers rode up. They sat down at the faro table and proceeded to lose their money—maybe a couple of hundred dollars. One of them whipped out his gun and covered the dealer, the other covered the lookout man. They raked in the entire bankroll, backed out, mounted, and fled. I learned later that one of the two was the notorious John Wesley Hardin, who was afterwards killed in El Paso. The name of his companion I never learned.

Further south, at the junction of the Black River and the Pecos, was Red Bluff, near which the Butterfield stagecoaches were held up so often that the government finally established a camp of soldiers near the point of the Guadalupes to protect travelers.

These are only a few of many happenings that gave the River of Sin its reputation, and it was against such a bloody background that Billy the Kid played his part as a fighting cowboy and became a legend to scare the papooses. The man himself was a good deal less of a fellow than the legend; and it's the man himself I mean to try to put together from the authentic pieces that are left.

The original published source material about Billy is contained principally in five books, as follows: Pat F. Garret, *The Authentic Life of Billy the Kid* (1882; 2nd ed., 1927); John W. Poe, *The Death of Billy the Kid* (1919); Chas. A. Siringo, *History of Billy the Kid* (1920); George W. Coe's autobiography, entitled *Frontier Fighter* (1934); Miguel Antonio Otero, *The Real Billy the Kid* (1936). It is significant that with the exception of Garrett's book, which appeared about a year after Billy's death, all of these have been published within the last twenty-one years, about forty years or more after Billy's death. For almost forty years the hero myth had little printed matter to feed on, and it was dormant or dying, and possessed only an antiquarian interest. Soon after the World War, however, the coals of interest began to show red again, and finally burst into flame. Old-timers, once given to obstinate silence about what they had seen, grew talkative, and began to tell what they remembered or thought they remembered.

The principal peg on which public interest was hung, of course, was the "fact," so called, that this beardless youth who died when he was little more than twenty-one, had killed "twenty-one men, not counting Indians"—a man for every year of his brief life. Armchair appetites demanded good stories about this matchless character, and supply has a tendency to follow demand in the fiction business as well as in the cow business. The stories became better and better, taller and taller, until maybe Old Truthful himself would be ashamed to own an interest in some of them. Old Truthful, I might say, was a character with a claim in the Guadalupe Mountains, who was famous for handling facts in a free-and-easy style. One of his stories had to do with a bear fight he allegedly fought with a huge old silvertip with an eight-foot tail. Attacked by Old Truthful himself, his little dog, and a swarm of bees all at once, the bear took refuge in a fifty-gallon barrel that Old Truthful had brought along to gather honey in. Her tail stuck out the bunghole, and Old Truthful tied a knot in it, thereby attaching the barrel permanently to her tail; and the bear left camp quick. The next time Old Truthful saw that bear, he said, was about a year later. She still had the barrel on her tail, and what's more, she had two cubs with her, and each one of them had a gallon keg in its tail.

"No, sir!" Old Truthful remarked after telling this yarn, "I don't go to town often. I like ter live up here. Yer see, there's a bunch that jest sets around the store with their feet wrapped around nail kegs, an' they're always tellin' lies. They make me so mad!"

Billy, the cow thief, the occasional killer, the buck-toothed desperado, became more and more a "hero" in the stories. Final deification came with *The Saga of Billy the Kid,* by Walter Noble Burns, a book in which a cook-up of fact and fiction was served with a literary sauce nicely calculated to please the palates of thousands of readers whose only range-riding was done in pipe smoke. There have been other publications claiming to give "the facts," which actually have only enhanced and embroidered the legend. That legend has now grown to such a size that it will not be ignored, even by those who know it to be about nine parts fiction to one part fact.

To appraise the substance on which this shadowy hero structure has been built, I have gone over all the evidence again, and here present results and conclusions.

II

Authentic knowledge of Billy the Kid, insofar as we have it, is confined to the last four years of his life. He rides out of the shadows of a nomadic boyhood, into the sunlight of intense and recorded action, in the year 1877. What he had done in the eighteen years of his life up to then, is largely conjecture. There is some evidence that Billy himself knew how to spin a good yarn about his past, and was not unwilling to have people think that he had done some pretty bloody and impossible things in the course of his travels. Many a cowboy did as much. And Billy seems to have known, as some women know, that "a past" can often be an asset—if you are not too explicit about the details. Many of the killings attributed to him are supposed to have taken place in that unlighted past, beyond proof or investigation. The story of that period is told, allegedly, in the first seven chapters of Garrett's *Authentic Life,* and most later writers have blindly followed his account, without recalling all of Garrett's reasons for writing the book.

It's a tall tale, as Garrett spins it. Before he was eighteen, Billy is credited with having ended the mortal agony of (a) a man who insulted his mother, (b) three Indians on the Chiricahua Apache Indian Reservation, (c) a "soldier blacksmith," (d) a monte dealer in Sonora, Old Mexico, (e) a monte dealer in Chihuahua City, (f) about fourteen Mescalero Apache Indians who had attacked an emigrant train, and (g) an uncounted number of Apaches near a spring in the Guadalupe Mountains. The flavor of these episodes, admittedly largely imaginary, is shown by the words attributed to Billy just before the Guadalupe Indian killings. To his lone companion, he is supposed to have remarked:

"I believe a little flare-up with twenty or thirty of the sneaking curs would make me forget I was thirsty while it lasted, and give water the flavor of wine after the brigazee was over."

That might be the way dime novels talk, but not cowboys.

During this period of his life, Billy is pictured as dropping in occasionally at towns where he was known, just to jeer at officers of the law who feared him, and "to watch their trembling limbs and pallid lips as they blindly rushed to shelter." But the author hedges occasionally on the authenticity of the events he is describing, for he says of one killing, "Billy never disclosed the particulars of the affair"; and of another, "The date and particulars of this killing are not upon record, and Billy was always reticent in regard to it." The truth is, of course, that Garrett was building up this desperado for purposes of his own. Sheriff Garrett, you remember, killed Billy in the dead of night, when out with two deputies to capture and return him to a condemned cell.

> A chance shot fired by Garrett,
> A chance shot that found its mark;
> 'Twas lucky for Pat the Kid showed plain,
> While Garrett was hid in the dark.

The West approved the kind of peace officer who gave even a desperate gunman a chance, and Garrett was always a little on the defensive in regard to the manner of Billy's death. His claim was, "If I had not shot him when I did, I would not be here to tell the tale." So he was interested in using any and every device he could find, to play Billy up as a super-gunman. In presenting an autographed copy if his book to Territorial Governor Miguel Otero (later the author of *The Real Billy*), Garrett said of his volume:

"Much of it was gathered from hearsay and 'made out of whole cloth.'"

Garrett himself, be it noted, did not do the actual writing of his book. That was the work of M. A. (Ash) Upson, an old newspaper man who is said to have boarded with Billy's mother in different towns. With a subject such as he had here, when he was not held down to earth by facts of which either he or Garrett had sober personal knowledge, Upson just loosed the bridle and let old Pegasus sunfish and windmill. Billy's name, he soaringly said, "will live in the annals of daring crime so long as those of Dick Turpin and Claude Duval shall be remembered. This verified history of the Kid's exploits, with all the exaggeration removed, will exhibit him as the peer of any fabled brigand on record, unequalled in desperate courage, presence of mind in danger, devotion to his allies, generosity to his foes, gallantry, and all the elements which appeal to the holier emotions."

That's pretty loud screamin' for *any* eagle!

I think it is permissible to dismiss as unproved, and probably untrue because incredible, most of the killings supposedly done by Billy before he became a participant in the Lincoln County War. What remains? There is a list of eleven killings, more or less charged against Billy in that strange uprising which helped plenty to brand the Pecos as the River of Sin. Did Billy do these eleven killings? And if so, were all or any of them "heroic"? Let's see.

(1) The first two of the eleven killings charged to him were those of Billy Morton and Frank Baker. The exact truth of the Morton-Baker affair will now never be known. It was one of the earliest incidents involving actual bloodshed in the Lincoln County War. The history of that war is much too complicated and obscure to dwell on in a single chapter here. It's enough to say that it was born of range and trade rivalries and involved what is known as the Murphy-Dolan faction on one side, and the Tunstall-McSween faction on the other.

The Murphy-Dolan faction was the natural one for a gunslinging tough like Billy the Kid to side with. Under the leadership of Jim Dolan, it represented political control and corruption, was allied with rustlers, grafters, and any who cared more about money than honesty. Such an outfit needed fellows who were prepared to steal cattle, blot brands, dry-gulch enemies, and otherwise do the devil's business on the range. And Billy did side with them. They were his first employers in Lincoln County. He played with their marbles, and maybe they paid him some wages. The big mystery is why he ever quit them for the other side. But quit them he did, and the reason may have been the personality of John Tunstall, the Englishman. Tunstall and Billy, somehow, seem to have been greatly attracted to one another right from the start, perhaps because they were such completely opposite types and their backgrounds were so different. Billy was a product of the raw frontier, and knew more about the inside of saloons, gambling halls, and *tendejons* than other kinds of inhabited buildings. Yet with it all he seems to have been possessed of a certain personal charm. Tunstall, by all accounts, was a cultured and educated Englishman of wealth. When they met, the spark of friendship was struck. George Coe tells of being in Lincoln one day, and asking Tunstall about Billy. He quotes Tunstall's reply:

"George, that's the finest lad I ever met. He's a revelation to me every day, and would do anything on earth to please me. I'm going to make a man out of that boy yet. He has it in him."

If these were not Tunstall's exact words, they undoubtedly reflect accurately his feelings, for Coe tells the truth about what he saw and remembers—and about what he didn't see, he keeps still. This remark of Tunstall's doesn't make a "hero" of the lad, but it does show him in a favorable light.

Now, the very first blood shed in the war was that of John Tunstall. He had come to Lincoln and opened a store which cut into the business of the store owned by the Murphy-Dolan crew, partnering in this and another enterprise with a man, Alexander A. McSween, who had displeased and defied that bunch. He had bought ranch interests and conducted himself on the range in an upright manner, which was calculated to bring him into conflict with their crooked operations. So, capping a series of events, Tunstall was waylaid and killed. Billy the Kid was working for Tunstall then. Just where Billy was at the time of this killing is a matter of dispute. He seems to have been just around the next hill shooting wild turkeys, but no one knows for sure. At any rate, the Tunstall killing was the shot heard round the range that set other Lincoln County guns to blazing.

Two days after the event, a group of Tunstall's friends carried his body to town. Four miles south of Lincoln, six Spanish-American workmen stood in a field of grain belonging to Señor Charles Fritz, and watched the procession pass. A youngster among them, Julian Chavez, listened to his elders (*hombres grandes*) discuss the event, and heard them express the opinion that it was an affair concerning American houses exclusively, and that probably the Mexican population would not be drawn into it at all. Many years later, in a naive longhand narrative recording his recollections of those days, Julian remarked that he himself of course had no opinion in the matter then, since he was a youngster and a young boy did not have opinions— *"Yo no tube opinion, pues estaba Joben, y las muchachas no tienen muchas opiniones."* But he discovered soon that the opinion of his elders was far from correct.

Bill Bonney and others swore vengeance on Tunstall's killers. The Lincoln County War was on, and nearly everybody in the region was drawn into it, either actively or passively, on one side or the other.

An unofficial posse, of which Billy the Kid was a member but not the leader, captured Morton and Baker, two men who were connected with the Tunstall killing. The posse started with them toward Lincoln, but the captives never got there. The story usually accepted is that for some reason they made a break to escape, presumably when one member of the posse, who was suspected of favoring their cause, was shot. Pat Garrett gives Billy the Kid all the blame for killing Morton and Baker. In one of these highly purple passages of his book, he (*via* Ash Upson) says:

"The Kid wheeled his horse. All was confusion. He couldn't take in the situation. He heard firearms, and it flashed across his mind that perhaps the prisoners had in some unaccountable manner got possession of weapons. He saw his mortal enemies attempting to escape . . ." And so on. "Twice only," Garrett dramatically declares, "his revolver spoke, and a life sped at each report."

Thrilling enough, if true. But it seems to be perfectly certain that Garrett was merely making up a good story, the way he wanted it, out of an event of which he had no first-hand knowledge, knowing that because of the peculiar circumstances, his account was not likely to be contradicted publicly by any of those who did have first-hand knowledge. George Coe, who knew Billy the Kid more intimately than Garrett ever did, said of the same event, "No one knows the details, but it is evident that . . . Baker and Morton . . . put spurs to their horses and made a desperate attempt for liberty only to fall, riddled with bullets, a few seconds later." He says that all the mention Billy ever made to him about the affair, was:

"Of course you know, George, I never meant to let them birds reach Lincoln alive." "Billy," he adds, "did not seem to want to talk about it."

Let's sum up. There were eleven members of the posse. All of them, except the prisoners, were heavily armed; the prisoners weren't armed at all, and they died. It requires a pretty big stretch of credulity to believe that when they fell dead, the only bullets in their bodies were those of nineteen-year-old Billy the Kid, who was not even the leader of the posse. In any event, were those killings the kind to make a "hero's" reader proud of him? Did they reveal the dash and daring of a resourceful, courageous soul endowed with "all the elements which appeal to the holier emotions"? Or were they more on the order of butchering a couple of range steers?

(2) Another allegedly daring killing laid at Billy's door was that of "Buckshot" Roberts. Garrett did not witness this killing either, but his hearsay account of it has a fine air of gallantry, dash, and derring-do befitting a knight of the range, a cowhand with lance atilt. The encounter took place at Blazer's sawmill. Once again Billy the Kid was a member of a large posse, and Roberts, the victim, was alone.

"As the party," says Garrett, "approached the building from the east, Roberts came galloping up from the west. The Kid espied him, and bringing his Winchester on his thigh, he spurred directly towards Roberts as Brewer demanded a surrender. Roberts' only reply was to the Kid's movements. Quick as lightning his Winchester was at his shoulder and a bullet sang past the Kid's ear. The Kid was as quick as his foe and his aim more accurate; the bullet from the rifle went crashing through Roberts' body, inflicting a mortal wound."

That's the way a "hero" and his worthy opponent ought to meet and do battle to the death! The only trouble is, that's not what happened; in fact, it's nothing like what happened.

George Coe was there. He and Billy the Kid were temporarily members of the same gang. His shattered right hand from which the trigger finger is gone, is evidence to this day of his participation in the Blazer's Sawmill fight. Dr. Blazer ran a sort of roadhouse, and the party of twelve men, one of them being Billy the Kid, arrived and ate lunch there, two of their number standing guard because they were expecting some trouble. While the main bunch was eating, trouble arrived— Roberts on a bay mule. The fireworks did not start at once. Roberts dismounted and told one member of the party, whom he knew personally, that he wanted to speak to him. They walked around the house and sat down in an open doorway. Meanwhile, others of the party conferred and decided that Roberts, who was known to be after their scalps for a reward that had been offered by the opposing faction, had better be "arrested." Dick Brewer, the party's leader, asked who would go around the house and get him. There were three volunteers, Charlie Bowdre, George Coe, and Billy the Kid, *in that order;* and in that order they started around the house, guns in hand and cocked. Bowdre called on Roberts to surrender.

"Not much, Mary Ann!" he replied. All the accounts agree that those were his actual words.

Bowdre had the drop, but Roberts and he fired almost simultaneously. "Bowdre's bullet," says Coe, "struck Roberts right through the middle, and Roberts' ball glanced off Bowdre's cartridge belt, and with my usual luck, I got there just in time to stop the bullet with my right hand. It knocked the gun out of my hand, took off my trigger-finger, and shattered my hand." Bowdre's bullet, and his alone, was the one of which Roberts died. But he did not die at once, and before he finally

90

passed out, he put up a very game fight. He took refuge in the room in the door of which he had been sitting, and from here he picked off and killed Dick Brewer, and wounded another member of the posse. Billy the Kid, according to Coe (who throughout his book tells only what he saw without elaboration), had slight part in the episode beyond being third in a party of three aiming to "arrest" Roberts.

Again the facts of a battle, in which one man was ranged against twelve, hardly seem to show Billy up as "hero" size.

(3) A third affair laid to Billy was a double killing—that of Sheriff Brady and his deputy, Hindman, on the main street of the town of Lincoln.

Garrett, who generally makes out a case for Billy's daredeviltry and courage when he can, calls this "a crime which would disgrace the record of an Apache." It occurred a few days before the killing of "Buckshot" Roberts. The sheriff of Lincoln County at that time was a certain Major Brady. All events of the Lincoln County War were backgrounded against a relatively passive and pacific, but by no means disinterested, native Spanish population; and their judgments of the principal figures involved in the conflict are not to be disregarded. Many of the Spanish people, for example, thought highly of Billy the Kid, and he is said to have liked them too, and it has been claimed that of all the people he is supposed to have killed in New Mexico, not one was a pure-blooded Spanish-American. Many of the Spanish people thought well of Major Brady, too. To quote once more from the manuscript of Julian Chavez, this sheriff was held by the Mexicans to be an honorable citizen and very much the gentleman (*muy caballero*), partly perhaps because he was married to a Mexican woman of the Bonifacia family. "I knew all of his family," Julian writes—"*yo conosi a toda su familia.*" However, Jim Dolan is supposed to have undermined the Major's sterling character simply by giving him a paid-in-full receipt for eight hundred dollars, to clear off the balance of the mortgage on the Major's home, and thereafter "*el buen hombre se doblego, y se presto a serbir ordener*"—the good man became deceitful, and put himself out to obey Murphy-Dolan orders without question.

"*Sabe Dios,*" exclaims Julian, "*Que tontas bacilasiones*"—God knows why men do such things!

Major Brady is supposed to have held warrants for the arrest of several of the alleged killers of Morton and Baker. So a group of the dead Tunstall's friends went to the town of Lincoln on April 1, 1878, and lay in wait for him behind an adobe wall surrounding Tunstall's store. They knew his habits, and expected him to ride along the main street at about the time they took up their positions.

How many lay in ambush behind the wall is reported variously. George Coe says there were five; others say there were eleven. One of them, at any rate, was Billy the Kid.

The sheriff failed to come past as expected. Hence, a man was sent to the lower end of town to pretend that he was drunk and shooting bottles off the shelves. News of this speedily brought the sheriff along Lincoln's one main street. With him were his deputy, George Hindman, and the clerk of the circuit court, Billy Matthews. As they passed the adobe wall, the ambushed "heroes" let them have it. Brady was killed instantly, Hindman lived barely an hour, and Matthews, though wounded, got away and lived to tell the tale.

Billy the Kid was credited with these murders. Garrett in

his book does not come right out and say whose bullets killed whom. He does call the murder "a most dastardly crime on the part of the Kid," leaving the hasty reader to conclude that Billy did it all, or at least engineered it. But Governor Otero reports Garrett as saying to him later that "he doubted if the Kid had even fired at Brady," giving as his reason that he hated Billy Matthews and would naturally have tried to get him first, and Matthews was the one of the three who got away!

We shall never know the truth. There was no science of ballistics then to measure bullet markings microscopically, and photograph them, and to say past all doubt that a certain fatal bullet came out of a certain gun. Did any bullet from Billy's gun come anywhere near any one of the three victims? Nobody can say for sure. Was his bullet only one of many that entered their bodies? Was somebody else's bullet straighter and more deadly? No one knows. But the nature of the crime speaks for itself. It was butchery from the ambushed protection of an adobe wall, and even a ruse was necessary to entice the victim to the spot. If that's "heroism," maybe somebody will be erecting a monument one of these days to every paid killer hired by Al Capone.

(4) Next we come to the killing of Bob Beckwith. I know of no reliable testimony denying that Billy did this killing. Most people think he did. Probably he did. The blood was shed in the turmoil of a general conflict.

Consider the circumstances. A major battle was fought between the two warring factions of the town of Lincoln, and was the culminating action of that war. Fifty or more partisans were engaged on both sides. The United States Army got into it too, in the person of a certain Colonel N. A. M. Dudley, commander of neighboring Fort Stanton, who seems to have acted in a role unlike that usually adopted by the Army. He came with a detachment of soldiers and a gatling gun, parked the military in the main street, and saw to it that the "right" side (the side he favored—the Murphy-Dolan partisans) got the breaks.

The McSween residence, in which Billy the Kid and a number of others held the fort, was fired and burned. While attempting flight from the burning building, Alexander McSween, who never carried a gun and did not on that occasion, was shot and killed. Beckwith, or Becues, an enemy partisan, rushed forward waving a pistol and yelling, so it is said:

"I killed McSween. I've won the reward."

"Yes!" cried Billy the Kid, who was still inside the burning building, "you won the reward all right." And shot him between the eyes, "killing him dead."

Maybe almost anybody under the circumstances would have done as much. Still, give the Kid all the credit the deed deserves.

(5) Billy was supposed to have added another notch to his gun by killing a bookkeeper, Morris J. Bernstein, employed at the Mescalero Indian Agency.

As Garrett tells it, Billy and a bunch of his pals rode up in plain sight of the agency and began stealing some horses, which in the nature of things was a fool thing to do. Bernstein witlessly said he would go and stop them, and though warned, tried it, and that sounds like another fool thing. To Bernstein's order to Billy to desist, says Garrett, "the only reply was from the Kid's Winchester."

Siringo copies the story from Garrett, and embroiders it, calling the killing the Kid's most cowardly act. Gratuitously,

Siringo adds that the Kid's excuse for shooting Bernstein had a strong Hitlerian flavor—"He didn't like a Jew nohow."

What were the facts? They seem to be perfectly clear. George Coe again was there, and has told the tale. He says that their party consisted of six or eight Mexicans, and four Americans—Hendry Brown, Billy the Kid, Fred Wayte, and himself. Their object, he affirms, was not horse-stealing, but to discover what had happened to the body of Dick Brewer, their former leader, after "Buckshot" Roberts had shot him in the battle of Blazer's Mill. When they were within a mile or so of the Indian Agency, Coe says, he and the other three Americans decided to go to the far side of the canyon for a drink at a spring. Now, the spring was out of the shelter of the trees, and the Mexicans, who were scared, refused to go. While the four were in the act of drinking, shots were heard. The four Americans mounted three horses, Billy's horse having run away at the first shot, and raced for cover. When they reached cover and came up with the Mexicans, they learned that a party of five riders had approached, and the Mexicans had desperately opened fire, killing one. The dead man was Bernstein.

"It is a matter of record," Coe points out, "that the Kid was accused of this killing, tried for the offense and acquitted. Several writers have attributed this murder to him as one of the most blood-curdling crimes of his career. Since I was present at the time, I can testify that he had nothing whatever to do with it."

So passes another "notch."

(6) Now we come to the sordid saloon killing of Joe Grant. Again the credit for the blood spilled, if it can be called any credit, seems justly due to Billy.

Grant was a Texas tough who apparently had it in for Billy, and Billy heard of his intentions and threats. One day Billy entered a saloon in Fort Sumner with a group of cowmen whom he had invited in for a drink. Grant was there already, and he was mean drunk. He made a lunge and grabbed a fine ivory-handled pistol from the scabbard of one of the men who entered with Billy, putting his own in place of it. Billy, who was ostensibly friendly with Grant, asked for a look at the pistol. Grant stupidly handed it over. Examining it, Billy saw that there were only three cartridges in the gun, and he whirled the chambers so that when next fired, the hammer would fall on a blank. He handed the pistol back to Grant, who thereupon got noisy behind the bar, began breaking the glassware, called Billy a liar, turned his gun on him, and pulled the trigger. Of course nothing happened, since the gun had been "fixed." Meanwhile, the Kid deliberately pulled his own gun, fired, and Grant fell dead.

Was this a "hero" act? Heroes supposedly fight fair. And these dice were loaded, so that Billy could hardly lose. Maybe Grant needed killing. But to me, the manner of his killing looks more like butchery than heroism.

(7) Jimmie Carlyle was a young blacksmith who had "hundreds of friends and not one enemy," according to Pat Garrett. "He was honest, generous, merry-hearted, quick-witted, and intelligent." And Billy the Kid killed him.

With three members of his cattle-stealing band, the Kid had been trapped by a posse in the roadhouse of Jim Greathouse. The posse called for a surrender. There was a parley, in the course of which Greathouse went to the posse for a talk, and stayed as a hostage while Carlyle, who was a member of the posse, went unarmed into the roadhouse to talk to the outlaws. It was agreed that if Jimmie was harmed in any way, Greathouse would be killed. Several hours passed. The time when Carlyle was to have returned passed. According to one story, some member of the posse fired a gun, and apparently Carlyle thought that Greathouse had been killed and his own life was now forfeit. Anyhow, he made a rush for the window, and leaped through it, taking sash, glass, and all. Billy fired at him, wounding him, and while he was trying to crawl away on hands and knees, Billy deliberately polished him off. During the melee, Greathouse escaped.

Again Billy's gun was notched by the murder of an unarmed, desperate man. The act of a "hero"?

(8) And now we come to Bell and Ollinger, Billy's last two killings—if he killed them both.

Pat Garrett, in the course of events, had been made sheriff. The main figures in the Lincoln County War had been killed off, and the "war" had degenerated into a ragtag-and-bobtail affair. Billy the Kid was now a notorious cow thief, a pest and a neighborhood blight, operating over eastern New Mexico and western Texas, and it was part of Garrett's job to get him and end the pestiferous pilfering. Garrett eventually captured Billy, very tamely, at Stinking Springs, and landed him in jail. Tried on the charge of murdering Sheriff Brady, Billy was convicted, and was sentenced to be hanged on May 13, 1881. He was lodged in an upper room in the old Lincoln County Court House, and because this building was a very poor excuse for a jail, Billy was leg-ironed and handcuffed, and was guarded day and night by Deputy Sheriff J. W. Bell and Deputy Marshal Robert W. Ollinger.

On April 28, a little over two weeks before he was to be hanged, Billy escaped. Both of his guards were killed.

How did it happen? Everybody knows the weaknesses and frailties of human observation. I read about a fatal automobile collision in which two newspaper reporters and a magazine editor, all trained to observe expertly, were passengers in the cars involved, yet there were seven different eyewitness versions of what actually happened, and no two were near enough alike to enable a jury to return a verdict placing the guilt. It is not strange that no one knows exactly how Billy made his escape, since the two guards were killed, and no one else is known to have been on the spot, and Billy, having flown, was not doing much talking for publication.

All stories, however, agree that Ollinger had taken some other prisoners across the road to supper, leaving Bell alone with Billy. Garrett's version is that Billy asked to be taken to the latrine, which was downstairs and outside in the jail yard. On the way back, he says, Billy ran ahead of Bell upstairs, broke into the room containing the jail's arsenal, obtained a six-shooter, and shot Bell who was coming up the stairs. Garrett doesn't say who told him that this was what happened—maybe he just "deduced" it. George Coe's version is that Bell and Billy were playing cards while Ollinger was away; that Billy dropped a card as if by accident, and when Bell stooped to pick it up, Billy drew Bell's gun from its scabbard and threatened him with it; that Bell made a lunge to escape, and Billy shot him. Charlie Siringo rather spectacularly claims that Billy had starved himself so he could get one hand out of his handcuffs, and that on the fatal evening Bell was facing him reading a newspaper; that Billy released his hand, swung the cuffs and stunned Bell, grabbed the deputy's gun, and shot him. Martin Chavez, a friend of the Kid's, is quoted by Governor Otero as saying that a line had been drawn down the center of the room and Billy had been warned to stay on his side of it; but he deliberately crossed over and taunted Bell, and when the latter was off guard, grabbed his pistol. Others, nameless, say that a confederate on the outside shot Bell, that Billy did not do it.

Be all that as it may, Bell was killed, and for lack of any eyewitness accounts, we can only guess and conjecture how it happened. Anyhow, Billy took advantage of his death. He next seized a double-barrelled shotgun, and fired both barrels into the body of Ollinger when the latter rushed across the street to see what was up. Billy then is said to have called for a file and a horse, and after freeing himself, made good his escape. No killings were credited to him after that. And less than three months later, on the night of July 13, 1881, he himself was shot to death in the dark by Pat Garrett in Pete Maxwell's bedroom in old Fort Sumner.

So the tale of the killings is told. What does it add up to? What must we conclude? Was Billy the brave lad and noble "hero" that he has been made out to be? Did he really kill as many men as he was reported to have killed?

I think not. Nowhere near as many. As I read the record, it is fairly certain that he killed the half-breed Beckwith, Grant, Carlyle, and Ollinger. Probably he killed Bell too. That makes five. I think some of his bullets may have lodged in the bodies of Morton and Baker, Brady and Hindman, but whether his bullets alone would have been enough to kill, no one can say. Definitely, he did not kill Roberts and Bernstein. Of the nine in whose killing Billy conceivably may have had some share, three were shot down when unarmed: Morton, Baker, and Carlyle. Two were killed from ambush: Brady and Hindman. One, Grant, was murdered after Billy had tampered with his victim's gun to make sure of an easy killing. That leaves three, and three only, whom Billy met on tolerably even terms: Beckwith, Bell, and Ollinger, and he killed them when his own life was in deadly danger. Such an analysis certainly removes a good deal of the glitter from the "hero" halo.

III

How, then, did the "hero" legend grow? In large part, apparently, it grew spontaneously out of the public's never-ending desire for a hero, and the mists and shadows that gather over all persons and events with the passing of time. There's a glamor about the cowboy's life, that is heightened by the thoughts of risks and dangers boldly met. It's hard to dramatize events without actors. Every play needs a hero. Billy the Kid has been cast in that role, and with the passage of time the facts have been distorted to make him fit the role according to the way we'd like to have had him be. Maybe the Robin Hood legends grew in the same way. Maybe a lot of "heroes" were just as insubstantial stuff in actual life. The Lincoln County War was a pretty sordid chapter in the history of the range, but it was nevertheless backgrounded against romance and color. There were hard-riding cowboys who were not afraid to fight hell itself for the lives and property of their friends, and the thought of them had always stirred the blood of arm-chair adventurers. Billy the Kid, a cow-country tough, happened to be enrolled on the "good" side in the Lincoln County War. He was admired by the likable and upright Tunstall. Perhaps his own insinuations about the unproved notches on his gun helped the stories about him to circulate. The fact that he died young was in his favor. The stories grew by what they fed on.

An important factor, too, was Pat Garrett. Probably a psychoanalyst would have a highfalutin word for him. I believe that Garrett felt a need to justify himself to himself and to the world. Governor Otero in a casual paragraph remarks: "In spite of the money and prestige which Pat Garrett secured for his services in killing the Kid, Tom O'Folliard, and Charlie Bowdre, the author has always felt that he regretted it."

Garrett and Billy had been good friends. But Pat killed Billy, and he was on the side of the law when he did it. As I said before, he always claimed that he had to do it; that Billy would have killed him if he hadn't killed Billy. But did Billy have a gun when Pat shot him? Pat always maintained that he did have. And John W. Poe, one of his deputies on that occasion, who later became president of the Citizen's National Bank of Roswell, in the reputable brief account which he wrote of Billy's death, said that Billy was carrying a six-shooter. But it was close to midnight when they met. The seeing wasn't good. Billy was admittedly in his stocking feet and almost completely undressed. And the first people to enter Pete Maxwell's bedroom after the shooting of Billy the Kid—Jesus Silva and an old Navajo Indian woman named Deluvina—both declared positively that Billy had no pistol.

Once more, who knows? The facts are clouded and the reports differ. Was Garrett secretly aware that he had shot an unarmed man? Did he purposely build up his victim in the book he sponsored and the stories he told, in order to justify himself? I knew Garrett, but I can't be sure of the answers to my own questions. Certainly he did build Billy up.

I first met Garrett at a wagon camp at the point of the White Sands, in New Mexico, when he came over to arrest a fellow. That was in 1889 or '90, eight or nine years after the dramatic killing of Billy. Garrett was a tall, slim, rawboned officer, with a black mustache and a very pleasant manner. I met him often afterwards at Santa Fe, Tularosa, Las Cruces, and elsewhere, and got to know him well. He was a rough-and-ready customer, a great lover of poker, with a good enough record in a hard line of work. He was made sheriff of Lincoln County on the theory that he would clean up Billy the Kid and other outlaws and cattle thieves; and he did that. But I have the impression that the rest of his life was haunted by ghosts from the Lincoln County War. In fact, it may have been one of these "ghosts" in the flesh that finally ended him, for he too died of a gunshot wound, under circumstances never fully explained. I think secret doubts about his own actions troubled him, and I believe he was driven to make Billy the Kid a more-than-life-size villain in order that Pat Garrett might be able to look Pat Garrett and the world straight in the eye. It's a curious and not impossible thought that he may have made the Kid a "hero," in order that he, the "hero" killer, might sleep easy at night!

IV

If he was not a "hero," then, what sort of chap was Billy the Kid?

We have the testimony of a lot of people that in certain moods he was a friendly and likable lad, with a sense of humor and a good singing voice, that he was undersized physically, with hands little larger than a woman's, a graceful dancer, polite and respectful to women, generally neat in personal appearance, and that he neither drank nor smoked to excess. Charlie Siringo met him at Tascosa, in Texas, in the late fall of 1878, when the Kid was over there disposing of a bunch of stolen horses, and Charlie writes:

"I found Billy the Kid to be a good natured young man. He was always cheerful and smiling. Being still in his 'teens, he had no sign of a beard. His eyes were a hazel blue, and his brown hair was long and curly. The skin on his face was tanned to a chestnut brown, and was as soft and tender as a woman's. He weighed about one hundred and forty pounds, and was five feet, eight inches tall. His only defects were two upper front teeth, which projected outward from his well shaped mouth."

George Coe says that when Billy bunked with him, most of one winter, he helped with all the chores and domestic work—"And I could not have asked for a better friend or companion."

Was he a wonderful shot? The testimony indicates that he was pretty fast with a gun, and coolheaded in using one in an emergency. Siringo has this to say: "While loafing in their camp, we passed off the time playing cards and shooting at marks. With our Colt's .45 pistols I could hit the mark as often as the Kid, but when it came to quick shooting, he could get in two shots to my one."

Garrett's testimony was somewhat similar. Asked by a newspaper reporter whether the Kid was a good shot, he replied, "Yes, but he was no better than the majority of men who are constantly handling and using six-shooters. He shot well, though, and he shot well under all circumstances, whether in danger or not."

George Coe, according to his cousin, Frank Coe, was the best shot among the Tunstall-McSween men. Frank Coe is quoted by Governor Otero as follows: "When he could take plenty of time for aiming, George hit the mark, and in hunting he always brought down more game than all the rest of the party put together. The Kid, however, was by far the quickest with a pistol; he could empty all six chambers of a revolver while an ordinary man was firing his first shot. He never seemed to take aim, but appeared to have an instinctive control."

George Coe, in the 220 pages of his book, makes little or no mention of Billy's shooting skill, except to say in one place that the Kid while spending the winter with him, did become quite expert as a deer slayer. Once at a shooting match, Coe tells, Billy was beaten by some buffalo hunters, and to get even with them, challenged them to a match with his friend— George Coe. Billy bet his last dollar on Coe, and won a dollar a shot until he banked eight dollars. If Billy had been a super-marksman, Coe undoubtedly would have mentioned the fact. His friends say he was good enough, but no wizard.

If he was likable, there are many things to show that Billy was not above saving himself at the expense of others, and in property matters he was shifty or worse. Siringo relates an exploit which he says was told him by the Kid himself. The government had given a gang of Mexicans a contract to put up a lot of hay at twenty-five dollars per ton. As they drew their pay, Billy who was an expert at monte, won it from them at cards. When the government contract was completed, Billy's source of money gave out, and he didn't like that. "With his own hands," Siringo says, "he set fire to the haystacks one windy night." The government had to let another contract at a higher price for more hay, and again Billy was on hand to win the money from the haymakers. There seems to be some reasonable doubt whether sharp practice of that kind is altogether "heroic."

Also, there are records of occasions when stolen cattle were sold, and Billy allegedly kept the bulk of the proceeds, giving his partners little or none of it.

And it seems as though Billy's action was deliberately despicable, or downright cowardly, on the night when his friend and partner, Tom O'Folliard, was shot and killed by Garrett's posse. Billy was riding to town with several friends. He sensed danger, and ducked. As George Coe, reporting the incident from hearsay, put it: "By a clever ruse he avoided them (Garret and his posse). He left his gang about a mile from town and rode in by another route"—leaving them to "take it!" Garrett's account of that incident is different: "With all his reckless bravery, the Kid had a strong infusion of caution in his composition when he was not excited. He afterwards told me that as they approached the building that night he was riding in front with O'Folliard. As they rode down close to our vicinity, he said a strong suspicion arose in his mind that they might be running into unseen danger.

"'Well,' I said, 'what did you do?'

"He replied—'I wanted a chew of tobacco bad. Wilson had some that was good and he was in the rear. I went back after tobacco, don't you see?' and his eyes twinkled mischievously."

A few minutes after going back for his chew of tobacco, thus taking his own hide out of the zone of danger, guns blazed out of the blackness, and the Kid's good friend, Tom, riding in front, received a mortal wound.

Billy, according to Garrett's report, declared that if ever he were taken prisoner by the law, it would be a dead man that the law got. "The Kid," says Garrett, "had sworn that he would never give himself up a prisoner and would die fighting even though there was a revolver at each ear, and I knew he would keep his word." Yet at Stinking Spring, after spending a cold night and day in an old stone shack, Billy and his three companions never fired a shot when Garrett and his posse built a fire and cooked supper outside. "The odor of roasting meat was too much for the famished lads who were without provisions. Craving stomachs overcame brave hearts."

No! Making all allowances, I think Billy the Kid was short weight for a hero. But the legend has grown past stopping. Even those who denounce him, now, merely add volume to his fame.

HISTORY OF "BILLY THE KID"

Charles Siringo claimed his first book, A Texas Cowboy *(1885), sold a million copies in his lifetime and was in print for more than forty years. His tell-all book on the Pinkertons was also a major success. No less important is his* History of "Billy the Kid," *with its contemporary account of the Lincoln County War and the murders of Sheriff Brady and Deputy Hindman.*

Siringo was an authentic Western lawman and Pinkerton detective and also one of the early chroniclers of the Old West. He was a participant in many of the events he describes and actually met Billy the Kid on a few occasions.

HISTORY OF "BILLY THE KID"

By Charles A. Siringo
1920

———•◦•———

CHAPTER IV.
THE STARTING OF THE BLOODY LINCOLN COUNTY WAR.
THE MURDER OF TUNSTALL. "BILLY THE KID" IS PARTIALLY
REVENGED WHEN HE KILLS MORTON AND BAKER.

Arriving back at the Murphy-Dolan cow-camp on the Pecos river, "Billy the Kid" was greeted by his friends, McDaniels, Morton and Baker, who persuaded him to join the Murphy and Dolan outfit, and become one of their fighting cowboys. This he agreed to do, and was put on the pay-roll at good wages.

The summer and fall of 1877 passed along with only now and then a scrap between the factions. But the clouds of war were lowering, and the "Kid" was anxious for a battle.

Still he was not satisfied to be at war with the whole-souled young Englishman, John S. Tunstull [Tunstall], whom he had met on several occasions.

On one of his trips to the Mexican town of Lincoln, to "blow in" his accumulated wages, the "Kid" met Tunstall, and expressed regret at fighting against him.

The matter was talked over and "Billy the Kid" agreed to switch over from the Murphy-Dolan faction. Tunstall at once put him under wages and told him to make his headquarters at their cow-camp on the Rio Feliz, which flowed into the Pecos from the west.

Now the "Kid" rode back to camp and told the dozen cowboys there of his new deal. They tried to persuade him of his mistake, but his mind was made up and couldn't be changed.

In the argument, Baker abused the "Kid" for going back on his friends. This came very near starting a little war in that camp. The "Kid" made Baker back down when he offered to shoot it out with him on the square.

Before riding away on his faithful "Gray," the "Kid" expressed regrets at having to fight against his chum Jesse Evans, in the future.

At the Rio Feliz cow camp, the "Kid" made friends with all the cowboys there, and with Tunstall and McSween, when he rode into Lincoln to have a good time at the Mexican "fandangos" (dances.)

A few "killings" took place on the Pecos river during the fall, but "Billy the Kid" was not in these fights.

In the early part of December, 1877, the "Kid" received a letter from his Mexican chum whom he had liberated from the jail in San Elizario, Texas, Melquiades Segura, asking that he meet him at their friend's ranch across the Rio Grande river, in Old Mexico, on a matter of great importance.

Mounted on "Gray," the "Kid" started. Meeting Segura, he found that all he wanted was to share a bag of Mexican gold with him.

While visiting Segura, a war started in San Elizario over the Guadalupe Salt Lakes, in El Paso County, Texas.

These Salt Lakes had supplied the natives along the Rio Grande river with free salt for more than a hundred years. An

American by the name of Howard, had leased them from the State of Texas, and prohibited the people from taking salt from them.

A prominent man by the name of Louis Cardis, took up the fight for the people. Howard and his men were captured and allowed their liberty under the promise that they would leave the Salt Lakes free for the people's use.

Soon after, Howard killed Louis Cardis in El Paso. This worked the natives up to a high pitch.

Under the protection of a band of Texas Rangers, Howard returned to San Elizario, twenty-five miles below El Paso.

On reaching San Elizario the citizens turned out in mass and besieged the Rangers and the Howard crowd, in a house.

Many citizens of Old Mexico, across the river, joined the mob. Among them being Segura and his confederate, at whose ranch "Billy the Kid" and Segura were stopping.

As "Billy the Kid" had no interest in the fight, he took no part, but was an eye witness to it, in the village of San Elizario.

Near the house in which Howard and the Rangers took refuge, lived Captain Gregario Garcia, and his three sons, Carlos, Secundio, and Nazean-ceno Garcia. On the roof of their dwelling they constructed a fort, and with rifles, assisted in protecting Howard and the Rangers from the mob.

The fight continued for several days. Finally, against the advice of Captain Gregario Garcia, the Rangers surrendered. They were escorted up the river towards El Paso, and liberated. Howard, Charlie Ellis, John Atkinson, and perhaps one or two other Americans, were taken out and shot dead by the mob. Thus ended one of the bloody battles which "Billy the Kid" enjoyed as a witness.

The following year the present Governor of New Mexico, Octaviano A. Larrazolo, settled in San Elizario, Texas, and married the pretty daughter of Carlos Garcia, who, with his father and two brothers, so nobly defended Howard and the Rangers.

Now "Billy the Kid," with his pockets bulging with Mexican gold, given him by Segura, returned to the Tunstall-McSween cow camp, on the Rio Feliz, in Lincoln County, New Mexico.

In the month of February, 1878, W. S. Morton, who held a commission as deputy sheriff, raised a posse of fighting cowboys and went to one of the Tunstall cow-camps on the upper Ruidoso river, to attach some horses, which were claimed by the Murphy-Dolan outfit.

Tunstall was at the camp with some of his employes, who "hid out" on the approach of Morton and the posse.

It was claimed by Morton that Tunstall fired the first shot, but that story was not believed by the opposition.

In the fight, Tunstall and his mount were killed. While laying on his face gasping for breath, Tom Hill, who was later killed while robbing a sheep camp, placed a rifle to the back of his head and blew out his brains.

This murder took place on the 18th day of February, 1878.

Before sunset a runner carried the news to "Billy the Kid," on the Rio Feliz. His anger was at the boiling point on hearing of the foul murder. He at once saddled his horse and started to Lincoln, to consult with Lawyer McSween.

Now the Lincoln County war was on with a vengeance and hatred, and the "Kid" was to play a leading hand in it. He swore that he would kill every man who took part in the murder of his friend Tunstall.

At that time, Lincoln County, New Mexico, was the size of some states, about two hundred miles square, and only a few thousand inhabitants, mostly Mexicans, scattered over its surface.

On reaching the town of Lincoln, the "Kid" was informed by McSween that R. M. Bruer had been sworn in as a special constable, and was making up a posse to arrest the murderers of Tunstall.

"Billy the Kid" joined the Bruer posse, and they started for the Rio Pecos river.

On the 6th day of March, the Bruer posse ran onto five mounted men at the lower crossing of the Rio Penasco, six miles from the Pecos river. They fled and were pursued by Bruer and his crowd.

Two of the fleeing cowboys separated from their companions. The "Kid" recognized them as Morton and Baker, his former friends. He dashed after them, and the rest of the posse followed his lead.

Shots were being fired back and forth. At last Morton's and Baker's mounts fell over dead. The two men then crawled into a sink-hole to shield their bodies from the bullets.

A parley was held, and the two men surrendered, after Bruer had promised them protection. The "Kid" protested against giving this pledge. He remarked: "My time will come."

Now the posse started for the Chisum home ranch, on South Spring river, with the two handcuffed prisoners.

On the morning of the 9th day of March, the Bruer posse started with the prisoners for Lincoln, but pretended to be headed for Fort Sumner.

The posse was made up of the following men: R. M. Bruer,

J. G. Skurlock, Charlie Bowdre, "Billy the Kid," Hendry Brown, Frank McNab, Fred Wayt, Sam Smith, Jim French, John Middleton and McClosky.

After traveling five miles they came to the little village of Roswell. Here they stopped to allow Morton time to write a letter to his cousin, the Hon. H. H. Marshall, of Richmond, Virginia.

Ash Upson was the postmaster in Roswell, and Morton asked him to notify his cousin in Virginia, if the posse failed to keep their pledge of protection.

McClosky, who was standing near, remarked: "If harm comes to you two, they will have to kill me first."

The party started out about 10 A. M. from Roswell. About 4 P. M., Martin Chavez of Picacho, arrived in Roswell and reported to Ash Upson that the posse and their prisoners had quit the main road to Lincoln and had turned off in the direction of Agua Negra, an unfrequented watering place. This move satisfied the postmaster that the doom of Morton and Baker was sealed.

On March the eleventh, Frank McNab, one of the Bruer posse, rode up to the post-office and dismounted. Mr. Upson expressed surprise and told him that he supposed he was in Lincoln by this time. Now McNab confessed that Morton, Baker and McClosky were dead.

Later, Ash Upson got the particulars from "Billy the Kid" of the killing.

The "Kid" and Charlie Bowdre were riding in the lead as they neared Blackwater Spring. McClosky and Middleton rode by the side of the two prisoners. The balance of the posse followed behind.

Finally Brown and McNab spurred up their horses and rode up to McClosky and Middleton. McNab shoved a cocked pistol at McClosky's head saying: "You are the s—of a b— that's got to die before harm can come to these fellows, are you?"

Now the trigger was pulled and McClosky fell from his horse, dead, shot through the head.

"Billy the Kid" heard the shot and wheeled his horse around in time to see the two prisoners dashing away on their mounts. The "Kid" fired twice and Morton and Baker fell from their horses, dead. No doubt it was a put up job to allow the "Kid" to kill the murderers of his friend Tunstall, with his own hands.

The posse rode on to Lincoln, all but McNab, who returned to Roswell. The bodies of McClosky, Morton and Baker were left where they fell. Later they were buried by some sheep herders.

Thus ends the first chapter of the bloody Lincoln County war.

CHAPTER V.
THE MURDER OF SHERIFF BRADY AND HIS DEPUTY, HINDMAN, BY THE "KID" AND HIS BAND. "BILLY THE KID" AND JESSE EVANS MEET AS ENEMIES AND PART AS FRIENDS.

On returning to Lincoln, "Billy the Kid" had many consultations with Lawyer McSween about the murder of Tunstall. It was agreed to never let up until all the murderers were in their graves.

The "Kid" heard that one of Tunstall's murderers was seen around Dr. Blazer's saw mill, near the Mescalero Apache Indian Reservation, on South Fork, about forty miles from Lincoln.

He at once notified Officer Dick Bruer, who made up a posse to search for Roberts, an ex-soldier, a fine rider, and a dead shot.

As the posse rode up to Blazer's saw mill from the east, Roberts came galloping up from the west. The "Kid" put spurs to his horse and made a dash at him. Both had pulled their Winchester rifles from the scabbards. Both men fired at the same time, Roberts' bullet went whizzing past the "Kid's" ear, while the one from "Billy the Kid's" rifle, found lodgment in Roberts' body. It was a death wound, but gave Roberts time to prove his bravery, and fine marksmanship.

He fell from his mount and found concealment in an outhouse, from where he fought his last battle.

The posse men dismounted and found concealment behind the many large saw logs, scattered over the ground.

For a short time the battle raged, while the lifeblood was fast flowing from Roberts' wound. One of his bullets struck Charlie Bowdre, giving him a serious wound. Another bullet cut off a finger from George Coe's hand. Still another went crashing through Dick Bruer's head, as he peeped over a log to get a shot at Roberts; Bruer fell over dead. This was Roberts' last shot, as he soon expired from the wound "Billy the Kid" had given him.

A grave yard was now started on a round hill near the Blazer sawmill, and in later years, Mr. And Mrs. George Nesbeth, a little girl, and a strange man, who had died with their boots on—being fouly murdered—were buried in this miniature "Boot Hill" cemetery.

Two of the participants in the battle at Blazer's saw mill, Frank and George Coe, are still alive, being highly respected ranchmen on the Ruidoso river, where both have raised large families.

After the battle at Blazer's mill, the Coe brothers joined issues with "Billy the Kid" and fought other battles against the Murphy-Dolan faction. In one battle Frank Coe was arrested and taken to the Lincoln jail. Through the aid of friends he made his escape.

Now that their lawful leader, Dick Bruer, was in his grave, the posse returned to Lincoln. Here they formed themselves into a band, without lawful authority, to avenge the murder of Tunstall, until not one was left alive. By common consent, "Billy the Kid" was appointed their leader.

In Lincoln, lived one of "Billy the Kid's" enemies, J. B. Mathews, known as Billy Mathews. While he had taken no part in the killing of Tunstall, he had openly expressed himself in favor of Jimmie Dolan and Murphy, and against the other faction.

On the 28th day of March, Billy Mathews, unarmed, met the "Kid" on the street by accident. Mathews started into a doorway, just as the "Kid" cut down on him with a rifle. The bullet shattered the door frame above his head.

Major William Brady, a brave and honest man, was the sheriff of Lincoln County. He was partial to the Murphy-Dolan faction, and this offended the opposition. He held warrants for "Billy the Kid" and his associates, for the killing of Morton, Baker, and Roberts.

On the first day of April, 1878, Sheriff Brady left the Murphy-Dolan store, accompanied by George Hindman and J. B. Mathews to go to the Court House and announce that no term of court would be held at the regular April term.

The sheriff and his two companions carried rifles in their hands, as in those days every male citizen who had grown to manhood, went well armed.

The Tunstall and McSween store stood about midway between the Murphy-Dolan store and the Court House.

In the rear of the Tunstall-McSween store, there was an adobe corral, the east side of which projected beyond the store building, and commanded a view of the street, over which the sheriff had to pass. On the top of this corral wall, "Billy the Kid" and his "warriors" had cut grooves in which to rest their rifles.

As the sheriff and party came in sight, a volley was fired at them from the adobe fence. Brady and Hindman fell mortally wounded, and Mathews found shelter behind a house on the south side of the street.

Ike Stockton, who afterwards became a killer of men, and a bold desperado, in northwestern New Mexico, and southwestern Colorado, and who was killed in Durango, Colorado, at that time kept a saloon in Lincoln, and was a friend of the "Kid's." He ran out of his saloon to the wounded officers. Hindman called for water; Stockton ran to the Bonita river, nearby, and brought him a drink in his hat.

About this time, "Billy the Kid" leaped over the adobe wall and ran to the fallen officers. As he raised Sheriff Brady's rifle from the ground, J. B. Mathews fired at him from his hiding place. The ball shattered the stock of the sheriff's rifle and plowed a furrow through the "Kid's" side, but it proved not to be a dangerous wound.

Now "Billy the Kid" broke for shelter at the McSween home. Some say that he fired a parting shot into Sheriff Brady's head.

Others dispute it. At any rate both Brady and Hindman lay dead on the main street of Lincoln.

This cold-blooded murder angered many citizens of Lincoln against the "Kid" and his crowd. Now they became outlaws in every sense of the word.

From now on the "Kid" and his "warriors" made their headquarters at McSween's residence, when not scouting over the country searching for enemies, who sanctioned the killing of Tunstall.

Often this little band of "warriors" would ride through the streets of Lincoln to defy their enemies, and be royally treated by their friends.

Finally, George W. Peppin was appointed Sheriff of the County, and he appointed a dozen or more deputies to help uphold the law. Still bloodshed and anarchy continued throughout the County, as the "Kid's" crowd were not idle.

San Patricio, a Mexican plaza on the Ruidoso river, about eight miles below Lincoln, was a favorite hangout for the "Kid" and his "warriors," as most of the natives there were their sympathizers.

One morning, before breakfast, in San Patricio, Jose Miguel Sedillo brought the "Kid" news that Jesse Evans and a crowd of "Seven River Warriors" were prowling around in the hills, near the old Bruer ranch, where a band of the Chisum-McSween horses were being kept.

Thinking that their intentions were to steal these horses, the "Kid" and party started without eating breakfast. In the party, besides the "Kid," were Charlie Bowdre, Henry Brown, J. G. Skerlock, John Middleton, and a young Texan by the name of Tom O'Phalliard, who had lately joined the gang.

On reaching the hills, the party split, the "Kid" taking Henry Brown with him.

Soon the "Kid" heard shooting in the direction taken by the balance of his party. Putting spurs to his mount, he dashed up to Jesse Evans and four of his "warriors," who had captured Charlie Bowdre, and was joking him about his leader, the "Kid." He remarked: "We're hungry, and thought we would roast the 'Kid' for breakfast. We want to hear him bleat."

At that moment a horseman dashed up among them from an arroyo. With a smile, Charlie Bowdre said, pointing at the "Kid;" "There comes your breakfast, Jesse!"

With drawn pistol, "Old Gray" was checked up in front of his former chum in crime, Jesse Evans.

With a smile, Jesse remarked: "Well, Billy, this is a h—l of a way to introduce yourself to a private picnic party."

The "Kid" replied: "How are you, Jesse? It's a long time since we met."

Jesse said: "I understand you are after the men who killed that Englishman. I, nor none of my men were there."

"I know you wasn't, Jesse," replied the "Kid." "If you had been, the ball would have been opened before now."

Soon the "Kid" was joined by the rest of his party and both bands separated in peace.

MIGUEL ANTONIO OTERO JR.
THE REAL BILLY THE KID

Miguel Antonio Otero Jr. was from an aristocratic family whose prop-
erty holdings in new Mexico dated to the old Spanish land grants. He
served as Territorial Governor of New Mexico from 1897 to 1906, and
as Treasurer of the territory from 1909 to 1911. Otero County, New
Mexico, is named after him.

Otero's description of events during the Lincoln County War and
Billy the Kid's role in the war is typically considered one of the more
interesting accounts. Otero makes a tragedy of Billy the Kid's life by
characterizing him as a hero who is slain by a lawless regime intent
on preserving the colonial relationships in New Mexico and destroying
Hispanic culture. This account is particularly valuable in its look at
the clash of cultures in the Southwest.

Excerpt From
THE REAL BILLY THE KID
With New Light on the Lincoln County War

By Miguel Antonio Otero Jr.
1936

———••◆••———

CHAPTER VIII
ECHOES OF THE LINCOLN COUNTY WAR

Such conflicting impressions and divergent opinions have been given in recent books about Billy the Kid and his part in the Lincoln County War that I am moved to publish some first-hand information gathered a few years ago from survivors of that time. The publication of Walter Noble Burns' *The Saga of Billy the Kid* had given renewed impetus to the romancing that has always enveloped The Kid and his exploits, and there was a revival of the legend that The Kid was not actually killed by Pat Garrett at Fort Sumner on the night of July 14, 1881. The legend was receiving embellishments at the hands of various persons as to how the fake killing was managed, how The Kid escaped to Old Mexico, and how he was still alive in some remote hiding place.

Just when I felt inclined to try to find evidence that would settle the matter once and for all, my good friend, Marshall Bond of Santa Barbara, California, and his son, Marshall Bond Jr., came to Santa Fé on a motor trip. When he learned of my interest in Billy the Kid he proposed that Mrs. Otero and I join them on a motor trip to the former haunts of The Kid. We readily accepted, realizing that we would be able to talk to a number of people in the vicinity of Lincoln and Fort Sumner who had been personally acquainted with The Kid and who were conversant with the events in which he figured. I shall now undertake to give an account of this trip and present in verbatim form, from the notes I made at the time, the information I was able to gather about The Kid and the Lincoln County War.

Our party left Santa Fé on the morning of Monday, July 5th, and as the roads were in excellent condition, we reached the town of Carrizozo (which we proposed to make the gateway of our journey into Billy the Kid's country) in the remarkably fast time of about six hours, although the distance was 176 miles. We spent the night at Carrizozo, and this gave us an opportunity to talk to George L. Barber, who, although well up in years, was still a practicing attorney. He had lived in Lincoln during the Lincoln County War, although he had not then begun to practice law. I believe he was then chiefly engaged in doing surveying. Somehow, Barber managed to preserve a neutral attitude during the Lincoln County War and was not identified with either faction. After things had quieted down, he married Mrs. Susan H. McSween, the widow of Alexander A. McSween. When I asked Barber what sort of a young fellow Billy the Kid had been, he replied: "The Kid was not half as bad as some of those who were after him and determined to kill him. I was in Lincoln the day The Kid escaped from jail, and I realized then that despite the fact he had killed his two guards, Bell and Ollinger, in making his escape, he had the community completely on his side. Outside of a very few—those belonging to the old Murphy-Dolan-Riley following—the community was sympathetic toward The Kid and the great majority was really glad that he made his escape. Hardly anyone believed he had received a fair and just trial, and they were glad to know that by his own ingenuity and nerve he had succeeded in getting his neck out of the noose that was, it was supposed, soon to close around it tightly."

When I asked Barber to tell me his impression of just how The Kid looked, he said: "He was a mere boy in appearance, always gay, jovial and high-spirited; but in an emergency he always stood out as a leader, quick, resolute, and firm."

The next morning we motored over to White Oaks, which is about twelve miles northeast of Carrizozo. White Oaks is now an almost deserted village, the railroad running far to the west of the place having brought about the death of what was, in the eighties, a bustling mining town with a population of three or four thousand inhabitants. Now comparatively few of the business houses and residences remain, and these give forth none of the hum of business or social activity. To be in the old town produces a decidedly melancholy feeling, particularly in the case of one such as I, who knew it in its palmy days and who had felt the lure of the golden metal that had brought the town into being. But the reason for including White Oaks in our itinerary was not so much to visit the remains of the town that had played a large rôle in the gold-mining excitement in New Mexico, as to make possible a call on Mrs. Susan H. Barber.

No one could meet Mrs. Barber, since dead, and not feel she was a very remarkable woman. Despite the fact that her life had been filled with eventful experiences, most of them nerve-racking and sad, she had maintained admirable poise and alertness. Even one who had not known her in younger days (and it was my privilege to know her when she first came to New Mexico nearly sixty years ago) could not fail to perceive in her aged face and form unmistakable traces of former beauty. When she came with her husband to New Mexico in 1875, she was a most vivacious and attractive woman. I recall vividly that she and her tall, distinguished-looking husband, Alexander A. McSween, made a couple that would have attracted attention anywhere. It would have been impossible to pass them without instinctively turning back to look at so handsome a pair. She was a descendant of one of the royal families of Germany, the Spenglers of Baden-Baden and justly prided herself on such noble ancestry.

As we talked together about the Lincoln County War, Mrs. Barber showed that the iron which had entered so deeply into her soul had not been altogether removed. Tears filled her eyes as she recalled and vividly related the occurrences of those perilous months.

I let Mrs. Barber give her recollections uninterruptedly, excepting for my questions. "Yes," she began, "I, of course, knew Billy the Kid very well. He came to Lincoln County some time during the year 1877 and shortly thereafter entered the employ of John H. Tunstall at his cattle ranch on the Rio Felice. Billy was a wholehearted boy—kind and loyal to all those deserving such a return from him. The best citizens of Lincoln County were his friends and admirers. He was universally liked; the native citizens, in particular, loved him because he was always kind and considerate to them and took much pleasure in helping them and providing for their wants. He thought nothing of mounting his horse and riding all night for a doctor or for medicine to relieve the suffering of some sick person.

"Billy was a graceful and beautiful dancer, and when in the company of a woman he was at all times extremely polite and respectful. Also while in the presence of women, he was neat and careful about his personal appearance. He was always a great favorite with women, and at a dance he was in constant demand; yet with it all, he was entirely free from conceit or vanity. It was just natural for him to be a perfect gentleman. I want to tell you a little story which will illustrate how much the natives loved him:

"One night a party of soldiers from Fort Stanton, working in the interest of the Murphy gang, was on the trail of Billy for some offense committed on the Mescalero Reservation. A party of Mexicans from San Patricio was responsible for the trouble, but as usual it was charged to Billy, and the soldiers seemed determined to get him dead or alive. The trail followed by the soldiers led to a small adobe house occupied by a poor Mexican and his wife. As the adobe had but one room, the man and his wife were sleeping on a mattress in one corner of the room, while Billy was sleeping on another mattress in another corner. The soldiers first surrounded the house and then pounded on the door for admission. Billy instantly crept to the bed in which his friends slept and whispered to the woman and her husband, both of whom immediately got up. Billy quickly lay down on their bed, and the man and woman covered him with his own mattress and bedding. They then lay down on the top of the newly made bed.

"When the pounding at the door was renewed, the woman got up and unlocked the door, asking: 'Who is there?' But before the soldiers could enter she got back into bed. When the soldiers piled into the room demanding to know if Billy was there both the man and the woman gruffly answered, 'No!' The soldiers looked around the room with the aid of lighted matches, and failing to discover signs of any person other than the man and woman, they finally gave up; and mounting their horses rode away. When they had gone, Billy reappeared from his place of concealment, though he was almost smothered to death between the two mattresses and the bedding. This was just one of his many wonderful escapes. His plans were always formed and executed as swift as lightning, no matter what the emergency. He never seemed to hesitate or to be at a loss—at least, on only one occasion—and that was the time he and Pat Garrett met in the room at Pete Maxwell's.

"The story I have just told illustrates also how loyal and faithful the native people were to Billy. They would harbor him even if a hundred warrants had been issued by the courts for his arrest. Billy was not a bad man; that is, he was not a murderer who killed wantonly. Most of those he did kill deserved what they got. Of course, I cannot very well defend his stealing horses and cattle; but, when you consider that the Murphy, Dolan, and Riley people forced him into such a lawless life through their efforts to secure his arrest and conviction, it is hard to blame the poor boy for what he did. One thing is certain—Billy was as brave as they make them and knew how to defend himself. He was charged with practically all the killings in Lincoln County in those days, but that was simply because his name had become a synonym for daring and fearlessness. When Sheriff William Brady was killed, we all regretted it, not that any of us cared much about the sheriff, but because of the manner in which it was done. Quite naturally the killing of the representative of justice turned many of our friends against us and did our side much harm in the public mind. Brady was killed by a number of bullets, being shot at by the whole bunch of men hidden behind the adobe wall of the corral in the rear of the Tunstall McSween store. I understood at the time that Billy said he tried to get Billy Matthews, who was walking with Brady, and did not even aim at Brady. I think his subsequent conviction for killing Sheriff Brady was based on insufficient evidence and was most unjust.

"Of course, Billy killed his two guards, Bell and Ollinger, but he was compelled to do it. Self-preservation is the first law of nature, and with Billy at that time, it was simply a case of killing both men and thereby saving his own life. He did not want to kill Bell, but Bell forced him to shoot. The killing of Bob Ollinger was approved by everyone, even Ollinger's mother, who told me that her son had been a murderer at heart from the cradle up to the moment of his death. She admitted that he got his just deserts when Billy shot him, giving at the moment evidence of unmistakable relish in doing so, had treated the poor boy so meanly that it was impossible for him to restrain his natural desire for revenge.

"Tom O'Folliard, one of Billy's associates, was another good-natured, rollicking boy, always singing and full of fun. He and Billy were much alike in manner, although Billy was far superior to Tom in every way. The truth is that Billy was quite alone in his class, and stood out as *sui generis*. I could not help liking the boy, although, as I said before, I did not approve of his mode of livelihood. It was the Murphy crowd who was to blame for his adopting this way of getting his living.

Mr. McSween did not approve at all of the killing of Sheriff Brady, and he told all of the boys implicated in it that he would do all he could to have them indicted for this killing. But I do not believe that if Billy had been given a fair trial it would have been possible to find him guilty of killing Brady. Of course he was in the party which did the shooting, and it is probable that he bragged about this fact, but on the other side is the fact that Brady was hand in glove with the Murphy faction, which was openly flaunting justice and law. In their effort to check the inroads that Mr. McSween and Mr. Tunstall were making into their schemes to get money by hook or crook, they deliberately planned the murder of both of them.

"Billy was generally accused of the killing of Bernstein on the Mescalero Reservation, but this was simply to get a United States warrant against him. I am convinced that he had absolutely nothing to do with the actual killing of Bernstein. The person who really did it was a small, deformed and mentally deficient Mexican boy named Isaacio Sanchez, who ran with Billy the Kid's crowd. Later on, Billy was forced to kill a man named Joe Grant, at Fort Sumner (I heard of it at the time) and all the circumstances indicated that the man Grant was responsible for his own death, since he had taken a hostile attitude toward The Kid. It seems that Grant wanted the fame that came with having killed The Kid, and went to Fort Sumner for that express purpose.

"Billy often told me that Pat Garrett was a cattle rustler and had stolen many a head of cattle from the Canadian while he was living at Fort Sumner. It was Captain J. C. Lea who got Garrett to turn traitor to Billy the Kid. For so doing Garrett was made sheriff of Lincoln County, the only condition being that he was to get The Kid, which he finally did in his usual way. Pat Garrett was much overrated as to bravery; he was a coward at heart and only shot when he had the advantage, or as they used to say, 'had the drop' on his opponent. It was said of Garrett that every man he ever killed was shot without warning, and I can well believe that this was the case. Garrett finally got what he most richly deserved at the hands of a young man, Wayne Brazil. I will say this much for Pat Garrett; he did have some fine children. His blind daughter, Miss Elizabeth Garrett, is a refined young woman, and in spite of her affliction, has succeeded in her study of music, having attained a national reputation as a vocalist.

"I have let myself get somewhat ahead of the order of incidents in the Lincoln County War. To go back to the commencement of the trouble, I should like to speak of the time the Murphy crowd poisoned one of the men who was working on the new store building for Tunstall and McSween. The Murphy men tried in every way to get our carpenter to quit working on the building, but with no success. So they resorted to other means. One day Nuff, the carpenter, was given a drink by one of the Murphy men, and in a few moments he dropped dead. It was very evident that he was poisoned but proof was impossible.

The Murphy gang stopped at nothing to accomplish their ends. They thought little of blackening the reputation of anyone who opposed and they did not scruple at taking away the reputation of a woman. I myself suffered at their hands in that way.

"I was in the house when the Murphy crowd set fire to it. Since the house was of adobe, the fire did not make rapid headway but instead slowly ate its way from the northeast corner around to the southeast corner. I would have remained in the house until the last wall fell had not the boys who were there with Mr. McSween insisted that I leave. I consented to do so much against my own desire. I did go back and forth between the house and Colonel Dudley's camp. I went to appeal to him to stop the wanton destruction of life and property that was going on. I found the colonel in his tent drinking whisky with John Kinney, one of the worst characters in the territory, a man who had been imported by the Murphy and Dolan faction and who, with Sheriff Peppin was the tool of that crowd. All three were intoxicated and used the vilest language while I was pleading with Colonel Dudley to save my burning home and the lives of those in it. John Kinney, in a very boisterous and bragging manner, told me that he had already killed fourteen men and would soon make it fifteen by killing A. A. McSween.

"The day after the house had been burned to the ground and five of those in it had lost their lives, several of the Murphy crowd went to the establishment of Tunstall and McSween and looted the store, carrying away thousands of dollars' worth of property.

"Billy the Kid often said that he loved Mr. Tunstall better than any man he ever knew. Just a few days before Mr. Tunstall was murdered, he told Sheriff Brady that he did not want any of his boys hurt either on his account or Mr. McSween's. I have always believed that if Mr. Tunstall had lived, The Kid, under his guidance, would have become a valuable citizen, for he was a remarkable boy, far above the average of the young men of those times and he undoubtedly had the making of a fine man in him.

"Matters continued in bad shape in Lincoln County for several months after the big fight in July, 1878, which is usually taken as the close of the Lincoln County War. My own life was in danger during practically all of that time. I had a great deal of responsibility on my shoulders in settling my husband's and Mr. Tunstall's estates. To aid me, I secured a Las Vegas attorney named George Chapman. He was a one-armed man but a fearless fellow. One night he arrived in Lincoln from Las Vegas, where he had been on business, and after stopping at the house where I was staying to bring me the good news that Governor Lew Wallace was strongly on our side of the conflict, he left to go over to his room, saying that he would return later. He happened to meet Jimmie Dolan, Billy Matthews and Billy Campbell just in front of the church. All three were armed with pistols and, what is more, they were all three drunk. Catching sight of Mr. Chapman, Dolan called out: 'Here is the scrub who is trying to stir up things again over the McSween business. Let's show him a trick or two.' Then he deliberately insulted Mr. Chapman, and the next instant the three bullies discharged their pistols against an unarmed man who only had one arm. Chapman dropped dead. The wretches then set fire to his clothing, thus destroying the legal documents in his pockets. All three of these men were indicted and tried for murder. Dolan swore he shot in the air; Matthews told the same sort of story; both were acquitted. Bill Campbell was found guilty but he afterward escaped from the guardhouse at Fort Stanton and was never heard of again. Of course his escape was all arranged. Dolan and Matthews were just as much guilty of murder in the first degree in the Chapman killing as Billy the Kid was for the killing of Sheriff Brady.

"Those were certainly terrible times. As I look back and think of all I went through, it seems a wonder I am here today. I really do not see how I escaped with my life. The hatred of the Murphy and Dolan crowd was turned most strongly in my direction, and several times their attempts at my life were only thwarted by my receiving timely warnings from some of my friends. As this crowd felt themselves protected by the powerful influences in the old Santa Fé Ring, they scrupled at nothing. No one will ever know the many horrible crimes which were committed, particularly in Lincoln and Socorro Counties that must be laid at the door of this group of villains.

"I would like to say one more thing. I wish to correct the statement made in Walter Noble Burns' book, *The Saga of Billy the Kid,* about my playing patriotic airs and other melodies on my piano while the fighting was going on about my house. I certainly would not have been so inhuman as to do such a thing while my house was burning and there was no knowing when a bullet might take our lives. We were all much too nervous and serious to think of playing the piano! Our only thought was—How are we to be saved?"

After saying adieu to Mrs. Barber and taking a few Kodak pictures of her in front of her home, we started back to Carrizozo, where we spent the night. The next day we drove over the steep Nogales Mountain and on to the old town of Lincoln, in the beautiful valley of the Rio Bonito.

MIGUEL ANTONIO OTERO
MY LIFE ON THE FRONTIER, 1864-1882

With a similar perspective to Miguel Otero's The Real Billy the Kid, *this account (published under his name without the Jr.) gives us insight into the capture of Billy the Kid by Pat Garrett and his posse at Stinking Springs, New Mexico, on December 3, 1880. He tells of a gunfight, and the killing of Billy the Kid's friend, Charlie Bowdre. Of the many accounts of Billy the Kid's capture, none is more authoritative. Otero also recounts his own father's honorable stand against a mob intent on vigilante justice. Otero admits he liked Billy the Kid, and nothing would have pleased him more than to see him escape, but it was not to be.*

MY LIFE ON THE FRONTIER, 1864-1882

Incidents and Characters of the Period when Kansas,
Colorado, and New Mexico were Passing through
the Last of their Wild and Romantic Years

By Miguel Antonio Otero
1935

I shall close this recital of the turbulent year 1880 with an incident near its end that caused Las Vegas to feel that it was participant in the lawlessness then rampant in the southern part of the Territory and that brought back to its notice Dave Rudabaugh.

Early on the morning of December 23, 1880, at the little rock house built many years before by Alejandro Perea, near Stinking Springs, N. Mex., Pat F. Garrett, Frank Stewart, Lon Chambers, Lee Hall, Louis Bozeman (alias "The Animal"), James H. East, Barney Mason, Tom Emory (known as "Poker Tom"), and Bob Williams (alias "Tenderfoot Bob") killed Charlie Bowdre and captured Billy the Kid, Dave Rudabaugh, Billy Wilson and Tom Pickett.

The Kid and his companions had taken refuge in the rock house when they felt closing around them the toils of Pat Garrett's determined effort to capture the party. Garrett's posse had besieged the rock house all during the night, and when Charlie Bowdre appeared at the door early the next morning, Garrett had given unmistakable indication of the temper of the quest, by shooting Bowdre, who died in a few minutes. So the Kid and the remaining three of his company decided to propose terms of surrender, which Garrett agreed upon, promising them protection until they could be tried.

In seeking a jail strong enough to hold the quartet, Garrett naturally turned toward Santa Fé, and as the nearest railroad station was East Las Vegas, he carried his prisoners there. The news that these noted desperadoes were coming through Las Vegas, and perhaps would be kept overnight in the Las Vegas jail, brought large numbers of curious people to the plaza.

Albert E. Hyde, who was in Las Vegas at the time, wrote a magazine article some years ago, giving a graphic eyewitness account of the entry of Garrett's party. As this tallies with what I remember, I shall reproduce it:

It was a beautiful afternoon, and the elevation of the Grand View Hotel afforded a wide range of vision across the plains, stretching to the blue line of distant hills.

As the hours passed, the crowds began to grow more impatient and distrustful. All had become skeptical, when from our point of vantage we discerned a cloud of dust in the southwest. When the cause of it advanced close enough for the people to descry a wagon outfit accompanied by mounted men, a mighty shout went up. The good news was indeed true. Billy the Kid was a prisoner and Pat Garrett was a hero.

As the wagon, pulled by four mules, approached, we saw four men sitting in the bed, two on a side, facing each other. The Kid, whom Dr. Sutfin had known in his cowboy days and instantly recognized, was on the hotel side of the wagon, chained to a fierce-looking, dark-bearded man who kept his slouch hat pulled well down over his eyes, and looked neither to the right nor to the left. This man was the daring and dangerous Dave Rudabaugh, who, among many other crimes, had killed the Mexican jailor at Las Vegas a short time before. He feared recognition, as well he might, for the Mexican population thirsted for his blood. The other two prisoners were Pickett and Wilson, prominent members of the Kid's gang.

Billy the Kid was in a joyous mood. He was a short, slender, beardless young man. The marked peculiarity of his face was a pointed chin and a short upper lip which exposed the large front teeth and gave a chronic grin to his expression. He wore his hat pushed far back, and jocularly greeted the crowd. Recognizing Dr. Sutfin he called: "Hello, Doc! Thought I'd jes' drop in an' see how you fellers in Vegas air behavin' yerselves."

Heavily armed deputies rode on each side of the wagon, with two bringing up the rear. Garrett rode in front. The large crowd evidently surprised and annoyed him. Fearing for the safety of Rudabaugh, he turned and gave a low order to the mule-driver, who instantly whipped up his team, and a run was made across the plaza to the jail.

Garrett heard enough during the next few hours to convince him that an attempt would be made to lynch Rudabaugh. He promptly increased his force to thirty men, who guarded the jail that night. In the meantime he planned to take the prisoners next day to Santa

Fé for safe-keeping. Not a suspicion of this move was allowed to get out.

Garrett placed his prisoners in the jail for the night. The next morning he began preparations to move them to Santa Fé by the railroad. But he experienced considerable trouble in getting the San Miguel officials to allow him to take Rudabaugh along, for local sentiment was strong for keeping the latter in Las Vegas now that he was back on the scene of his crime. Garrett protested that he held his prisoners under a United States warrant and that this fact gave him a precedence over the local officials. But the Las Vegas officers were not inclined to yield.

Finally, despite the mutterings of the Las Vegas people, Garrett placed the four prisoners in a closed carriage and hurried them to the railroad depot in the New Town, where he found a mob assembled, the majority of whom were armed with rifles and pistols. Sympathetic with the mob were the sheriff, Desiderio Romero, and his deputies, headed by his brother, Pablo Romero, generally called "Colorow" on account of his red hair and heavy, bushy, red mustache and chin whiskers. The demand that Dave Rudabaugh be turned over to the Las Vegas officers was renewed, and again Garrett refused.

He had managed by this time to get his prisoners aboard the train and had them in one car under a heavy guard consisting of Cosgrove, Stewart and Mason. The mob surrounded the depot and train, and showed signs of forcing its way into the car where the prisoners were held. But Garrett stood on the platform, calmly, and said: "I promised these men I would deliver them to the sheriff of Santa Fé County or to the United States officer at Santa Fé, and I intend to do exactly as I promised. Now, if you people insist on trying to take them away from me, I can see only one thing for me to do and that is to arm every one of them and turn them loose to defend themselves as best they may. And what is more, all my officers and myself will assist in protecting them."

As Garrett finished talking, my father got up on the car-platform and stood beside him. He first shook Garrett's hand, and then turning to the sheriff and his deputies, as well as to the mob, said: "Gentlemen, these prisoners are in the custody of Mr. Garrett, and he has given his word that he will turn them over to the proper authorities at Santa Fé. This I know he will do. Now, it is a very serious thing for you men to hold up the United States mail as you are doing, and as the train is ready to start, I appeal to you, as your friend, to retire at once; otherwise the consequences may be very severe. I will give you my personal guaranty that Mr. Garrett will do exactly as he has said. The judge of this judicial district resides in Santa Fé, and on their arrival there, he will immediately take full charge."

This speech had the desired effect. The officers and the mob withdrew, and the train, which had been held up for about an hour, pulled out on its way to Santa Fé. While the mob was holding the train and seemed determined to take Rudabaugh away from the officers, Pat Garrett stepped back into the car. To the prisoners Garrett said: "Do not be uneasy. We are going to fight if they try to enter this car, and if the fight comes off I will arm you and allow you to take a hand." Rudabaugh was excited and considerably worried, but not so Billy the Kid. At Garrett's promise, the Kid's face beamed and his eyes fairly glistened, and he replied: "All right, Pat; all I want is a six-shooter. There is no danger though; those fellows won't fight."

I really believe, however, that the Kid was disappointed that the mob did not attack the car, for it would have unquestionably resulted in an opportunity for him to escape. Undoubtedly he had many friends among the crowd, for it was well known that he was on good terms with the native element of the country and had protected and helped them in every possible way. In return the native citizens were ready to do all in their power to assist him. If there had been an attack, the chances are that Garrett and his companions would have been killed in their effort to keep their prisoners. Rudabaugh would have fallen into the hands of the mob, and possibly lynching would have followed. But the quick and elusive Kid would probably have lost himself in the crowd and disappeared from the scene. My brother and I were so much interested in the whole thing that we secured permission from my father to go along on the train to Santa Fé, and we enjoyed ourselves immensely in the company of Garrett and his guards and their prisoners. On the way over, we talked much with Billy the Kid and Rudabaugh. The latter we knew quite well, as he had been on the police force in East Las Vegas for a time together with Mysterious Dave Mathers. The Kid we had never seen before, though we were of course familiar with his part in the Lincoln County War and in the reign of terror he had afterward created.

During our stay in Santa Fé, we were allowed to visit the Kid many times at the jail, taking him cigarette papers and tobacco, as well as chewing gum, candy, pies and nuts, for he was very fond of sweets and asked us to bring him such things. My impression of the Kid was that he was just about the same, so far as general appearance went, as most boys of his age. Sitting very close to him in the railroad coach, I observed quite plainly his apparent interest in everything taking place inside and outside of the car in which we were riding. He seemed to be intent on some weighty matter involving himself, and possibly was at the time evolving plans as to what to do in the event of an attack by the mob.

To be frank, I found myself liking the Kid, and long before we had reached Santa Fé, nothing would have pleased me better than to have witnessed his escape. He had his share of good qualities: he was pleasant to meet; he had the reputation of always being kind and considerate to the old, the young, and the poor; he was loyal to his friends and, above all, loved his mother devotedly. He was simply unfortunate in starting life, and became the victim of circumstances. I had been told that Billy had an ungovernable temper; if so, I never saw it in evidence, for he was always in a pleasant humor when I happened to meet him. Mrs. Jaramillo at Fort Sumner said of him: "Billy was a good boy, but he was hounded by bad men who wanted to kill him, because they feared him, and of course he had to defend himself." Don Martin Chaves of Santa Fé said: "Billy was a man with a noble heart, and a perfect gentleman. He never killed a native citizen of New Mexico in all his career, and the men he killed, he simply had to in defense of his own life. He never had to borrow courage from any man as he had plenty of it himself. He was a brave man and did not know what fear meant. They had to sneak up on him at dead of night and then murder him."

Mrs. Jaramillo I have known for many years. She is a lovely woman, kind and gentle. Don Martin Chaves is a quiet, unassuming and kindly gentleman. He is well up in the seventies and is in perfectly good health today. Most of the older citizens of Santa Fé are well acquainted with him, and he holds the respect and esteem of everyone knowing him in his community. So the testimony of these two regarding the real character of the Kid carries considerable weight. My own personal impression corroborates that of these other persons. In looking back to my first meeting with Billy the Kid, I have no hesitancy in saying my impressions of him were most favorable ones, and I believe I can honestly say he was "a man more sinned against than sinning."

Dave Rudabaugh remained in jail at Santa Fé for a time and was then taken back to Las Vegas and tried for the killing of Antonio Lino, the jailor. The outcome was conviction and a sentence to be hung, but Rudabaugh escaped from jail and went to Old Mexico, where he got into serious difficulty by killing a Mexican officer. The man whom he killed was very popular, and his friends went after Rudabaugh in great numbers and with more success than did the friends of Lino. They finally surrounded him, and in the fight that ensued, Rudabaugh was killed. His head was cut off and carried on a long pole around the Mexican plaza where Rudabaugh's victim had lived. After this display, the head and the body were given to the vultures to devour, and the well-picked bones left to bleach on the hillside. Grim as was this ending, I am inclined to think it was deserved, for Rudabaugh was one of the most desperate men of those wild days.

SHERRY ROBINSON
BILLY THE KID

Eve Ball, a teacher, writer, and historian, lived near the Mescalero Apache Reservation for many years, striking up friendships with many members of the tribe. Another side of Billy the Kid is seen in her collection, Apache Voices. *It turns out that the Apache did not revel in their role in the Lincoln County War, and Billy the Kid was not a friend to them. They were mystified then, as many are now, by the lawlessness of the period.*

Sherry Robinson is an editor, journalist, and freelance writer who has resurrected Eve Ball's work.

APACHE VOICES
Their Stories of Survival As Told to Eve Ball

By Sherry Robinson
2000

———•◦•———

A t Fort Stanton Billy the Kid was making a raid on the Indians all the time for their horses," said Percy Big Mouth. "We made a big brush corral at Fort Stanton right near the fort. We got a brush corral and to protect us against Billy the Kid. One night they came over, tore all the brush down and got all our horses. The soldiers would go after Billy."

Two incidents and three murders of the much-chronicled war took place on the Mescalero reservation. One was the battle at Blazer's Mill, on 4 April 1878. The second occurred on 5 August. Billy, with a party of some twenty Regulators (Tunstall men), rode onto the reservation. While part of the group stopped at a spring, the rest continued toward the agency and, when they encountered Apaches, began firing. Agent Godfroy and his clerk, Morris J. Bernstein, were doling out rations but at the sound of gunfire, sprang to their mounts and rode out. Bernstein, in the lead, was shot down and Godfroy turned around and hurried back to the safety of the agency. The Regulators made off with all the horses and mules in the agency corral.

Again, the recollection of eyewitnesses is different from existing accounts. Mescaleros say there were just three rustlers—Frank and George Coe and Billy.

Leroy and Darlene Enjady said during an interview, "My grandmother saw Billy the Kid and his gang ride down the road from the east and turn off there at the old trail near the spring. She went on to the trading post, which was about where the old post office stands now. There was a hill between them and the spring. A man came into the agency to report that the White Eyes were stealing the Apaches' cattle. Bernstein took a saddled horse at the hitch rack and rode over the hill. In a few minutes they heard the shots that killed him but it was a half hour or so before anybody went to investigate."

"Dad was here when Billy the Kid's bunch killed Bernstein," Percy Big Mouth said. "This happened on Saturday when Billy's bunch came over from the North Fork and [some Mescaleros] were getting their rations and they saw a cloud of dust above the agency and knew somebody must be doing something. They told it to the office and the chief clerk said, 'I will tell them not to come. I will send them back.' He got his rifle.

"'Wait 'til we get our rations and let them alone.'

"'No, they will mind me.'

"'No, they outlaws. They will not listen.'

"Peso told the clerk to wait until they got their rations. Then they would send their women away and the men would go with him but Bernstein said he could handle them. So he rode up there and put himself just north of the present office just about 200 yards. The outlaws came up on the hill.

"'You go back.'

"'Who said so?'

"'I am saying so.'

"And they shot him right then. Some Indians got on their horses and rode around where the Catholic Church is now and got some horses away from the outlaws.

"The Indians said that when they killed that clerk two men jump off and search that fellow and took his gun and they got two of those horses."

Another comment suggests that if Bernstein had been less impulsive, he might not have died. Bessie Big Rope recalled, "When Bernstein was killed the Indians were prepared to ambush the horse thieves."

"In the minds of many people the killing of Bernstein was a sequel to the Roberts-Brewer fight," Eve Ball wrote in a note attached to a letter from Paul Blazer. While history remembers Bernstein as one more shooting among many of the Lincoln County War, the Apaches remember their own people who paid with their lives when Billy the Kid and his gang wanted their horses.

Percy Big Mouth said, "One hundred yards from the office these two went over a little hill. . . . Just over this side Eclode's mother was gathering her horses and hobbling them. Next morning she went after her horses again and the outlaws came down here gathering up horses, all they could find. This woman hobbled her horses and saw them up on a hill. Probably they wanted to take the horses but the woman got mad and tried to fight. And one of those outlaws shoot and killed her and take her horses.

"Same thing happen down Round Mountain right near Nogal Canyon. Billy's gang came and shoot the camp up. One woman still in the tipi. They see her shadow and shoot and kill the woman. They took her horses and left. And Crook Neck know about it too. One Saturday the horses [were] by the cemetery. This gang came and saw the horses. They cut the hobbles and drive them off. 'The broad hat people steal our horses and drive them away.' They mean Billy the Kid's gang."

On 7 November, agent Godfroy asked his superiors if he could organize an Indian police force. Between the lingering Lincoln County War and other crime on the reservation, the Mescaleros were too frightened to stay near the agency and camped instead in small groups at a distance. They were particularly upset about the murder of Bernstein. "In that last council the Indians demanded that if they organized as police that they should be armed with Winchester rifles, which, of course I would not permit," he wrote. The Mescaleros did ultimately get a police force but the fear of Billy lingered, even after he was gunned down by Pat Garrett.

Said Eric Tortilla, "I worked with Mexicans over here in a logging camp in 1920 who told me that Billy the Kid was still living."

KIT KNIGHT
WOMEN OF WANTED MEN

In her compelling and artful collection Women of Wanted Men, *widely-published poet Kit Knight imagines the world of Billy the Kid through the eyes of some of the women traditionally associated with his story.*

Ms. Knight is a widely published poet, whose other books (with husband, Arthur Knight) include The Beat Road, The Beat Journey, *and* Kerouac and the Beats.

POEMS FROM
WOMEN OF WANTED MEN

By Kit Knight
1994

CATHERINE BOUJEAU, THE KID'S MOTHER: 1874

I named my son Bill, after
his father. My Billy was born
in New York, but conceived in
the sultry air of New Orleans.
Bill was the first man
I met when I got off
the boat from Jamaica. My dad
offered to buy a business—
up north—for Bill, if
he'd marry me. Up there,
Bill found a grave. Another man
shot him. Over me. Baby Billy
was only three as he watched
his daddy take seven days
to die. The child's smiles
were desperate. After the funeral,
another man wanted to take me
to Kansas. He told me
he owned land there. After
one night, I never saw him
again and nine months later
Billy had a brother. I took

my sons west. In Wichita,
I owned a laundry and my hands
were always red and chapped.
Bleeding. Billy
was 13 and made no secret
of not liking his new daddy
when I married again. We moved
to New Mexico, hoping
the dry air
would help. I bleed if
I breathe deeply and it's
been over a month
since I left my bed. Billy
frets. Waits. Watches
my tortured breathing. He's
a boy of action. I watched
as he threw a heavy chair
at Mr. Antrim and knocked
my husband out. As I listen—
trying not to breathe—
to birds singing hard enough
to tear their throats out,
Billy holds my hand and
smiles. Desperately.

THE REVEREND'S WIFE: 1878

It's my duty to be a good
cook; I'm supposed to correct
the injustices of the world

with beans. Billy always
insists on coffee. Most folks
refuse to believe
Billy the Kid never touches
whiskey. I've seen all the men
on the New Mexican frontier
—including my Presbyterian
husband—so drunk they walked
on their knees. But never
Billy. My newest duty
requires me to play the organ
while my husband delivers
a eulogy in a voice guided by
wing beats. The dead man
owned a ranch that employed
fifty men, but they weren't
enough. This is a land
saturated in blood.
A bullet smashed into
Mr. Tunstall's head and
another "dusted" both sides
of the Englishman's elegant
jacket. The cowards murdered
his horse, too. Billy, 17,
was on a hill chasing
a turkey for dinner. Close
enough to see, but too far
for his awesome skills
to help. I've seen Billy
twirl pistols in opposite

directions and have both
come up cocked and able
to shoot off a burning
cigar ash. I've seen Billy
on a racing mare, bend
and fire under the bay's belly,
blowing the head off
a snowbird. Billy's Winchester
can shatter a man's leg
or his spine
at a quarter mile. When the Kid
looked at his friend's body,
he said, "I'll get some of them
before I die." The war
for Lincoln County had begun.

SALLIE CHISUM, 1878: CLEAR LIGHT
At 16, I've spent half my life
watching boys show off
for me. This summer is serious;
I'm managing Uncle John's house
and presiding
over a table set for
twenty-three. My uncle is
Cattle King of New Mexico
Territory; 80,000 Chisum cows
range part of Lincoln County.
And that county alone
is as big as South Carolina.

Skies in the west
are huge. Back home,
there's nothing like this.
Western stars are painted
with magic. I'd heard stories
about outlaws. Billy the Kid
shot men between the eyes
at 30 feet and never
flinched. Silhouetted
by a sun so bright it was
as if someone had shot
the day off in my face,
I watched Billy race
his mare and casually lean
from his saddle to scoop up
cosmos,
the showy daisy. He came in
wearing a six-gun on his hip
and carrying a Winchester and
I didn't need to know
who this boy was to know
what he was. During the War,
hundreds of reckless rebs
behaved as if they were
in search of death. As Billy
removed his hat and handed me
the flower, he said, "I'm not
as bad as they say; newspapers
have me a half-animal." I was
stunningly aware

Billy's body was graceful and
slim as clear light. Almost
pleading, Billy added,
"A gunfighter ain't nothin'
but a man."

MRS. SCOTT MORRE, 1879

My hotel serves the best dinners
in New Mexico Territory and
Billy the Kid is a frequent
guest. He always rides in
sharing his saddle
with a small dog. My husband
went to school with Jesse James
and when the bandit considered
leaving his past and settling on
a ranch, he wrote to Scott
for help. A month later,
the outlaws met. At first,
Jesse was introduced as
Mr. Howard, a train inspector.
Later, a private meeting
was arranged. Billy was
thrilled—
the two most feared men
in the west were in the same
room—and suggested they team up
and turn America
inside out. Jesse, more than

a decade older, said he was
tired of being hunted and only
wanted a home. A safe place.
Jesse's wife was expecting
another baby. Billy
had babies, too,
and waved his hand
in dismissal. So what?
Mr. Howard was amused
the teenager called himself
a man. Billy showed us
his newest trick. He'd trained
the dog to sit still
while Billy tore up the ground
around the whimpering animal
with his pistol. How close
could he come
without making the dog
bleed? I'd seen Billy do this
with drunks. He'd give the man
a bottle if he promised
to hold still. Once,
Billy grazed an old sot's nose.
As Jesse watched, he said,
"That boy will never see 21."

MANUELA BOWDRE, CHRISTMAS DAY 1880
Billy speaks my language;
not many Anglos can

speak fluent Spanish. Not many
want to. The tall white men
only want our land and
they take it. Might may not
make right, but it sure makes
what is. My Charlie has been
dodging the law, for years,
with Billy the Kid. The boy
can talk to me
better than Charlie. Gossips
in the village say the Kid
does things with me that
only Charlie
should be doing. But Billy
with his smiling blue eyes
is as welcome in adobe huts
all thru New Mexico Territory
as he is in mine. Many
Spanish girls are proud to be
Billy's *querida,* his love. Even
for a short time. Abrana just
had Billy's second child and
everyone knows
Billy also fathered
Nasaria's daughter. Wearing
Billy's hat, my Charlie stepped
out of the rock house and
Sheriff Pat Garrett shot him.
Carefully aiming, Garrett also
dropped a horse so as

to block the door. Billy
had to surrender; he was chained
to the wagon that carried
my husband's body. Tracks
in the snow. In English,
Garrett told me Charlie's
last words were, "I wish . . .
I wish . . ." But he fell before
he could finish. With all
my baffled rage, I slapped
Garrett. Punching him. Hard.
My arm hurt.
Shackled, Billy shouted,
"*El murio aspirando su nombre.*"
"He died breathing your name."

PAULITA, 1881: WIDOW

Fifty men were involved in
the Lincoln County War and
all 50 were rustlers and
murderers, but only
Billy the Kid was
convicted. Shackled,
he was brought to my home
after his capture at
the house of rock. Candles
glowed. It was Christmas and
I wanted the chains taken off
so Billy and I could go

in the bedroom and talk. But
the deputies were afraid,
probably, with cause. Billy
kissed me and the only talk
that mattered
was conducted between our
trembling bodies.

I'm going to have this man's
nino. I know there were
other women, other babies.
But this one shares
my body. Billy has to live
for his son. For me.

Five months later,
newspapers were headlined
"A Spectacular Escape
By New Mexico's Premier
Outlaw." The Kid rode away
despite handcuffs, leg-irons
and two guards. Billy shot
both. The total is now four
dead men. And Billy took part
in the deaths of six others.
Still, far from the 21 murders
papers heap on Billy Bonney's
slim shoulders. The bad image
is a newspaper creation.
Billy is a wanted man—$500

is on his head—and he wants
to marry me. And I love a man
who leads an impossible
life. I will be a widow
before I am a wife.

CELSA, 1881: THE YEAR THE STARS FELL

I was married when I met Billy
the Kid. Sabal didn't like
the Spanish speaking Anglo
around. The first time Billy
approached me, he wasn't
drooling; many men, particularly
those with a reputation,
believe they can always
buy the night. Billy came
to me at dusk. A magic time.
I could almost
see the air. He carried
his hat in his hand and said
women carry their brains
and their hearts
in their hands and wished
he were that smart. He said he
was going to marry Paulita,
but not tomorrow. New Mexico
is assured statehood if
lawlessness will end, an awesome
task. The postmaster for

Lincoln County has wanted bills
for over 5,000 men. But Billy
is best known. Pat Garrett
was a buffalo hunter and
a bartender, but he
rode with Billy and knows
exactly where
the Kid stays. Solely
on that basis, Pat was elected
sheriff by the landowners.
I know I owe my loyalty
to my blood. Pat is married
to my sister. I am married.
But Sabal doesn't give the stars
my name. It was a night
when the darkness was so thick
I almost heard it separating
as Billy left my bed
to look at stars and
shadows. Two shots
blew holes thru the quiet.
Sabal was on the coroner's jury
that declared Garrett's
traitorous shot-in-the-dark
"justifiable homicide."

JOHNNY D. BOGGS
LAW OF THE LAND

This modern reconstruction of the historical events leading up to and including the trial of Billy the Kid for the murder of Brady and Hindman is based on the best historical evidence available to Boggs, a highly prolific author and three-time Spur Award winner from the Western Writers of America.

When Billy finally comes to trial for the killing of Brady and Hindman, he realizes, perhaps for the first time, that he is doomed.

EXCERPTS FROM

LAW OF THE LAND
A Guns and Gavel Novel

By Johnny D. Boggs
2004

CHAPTER 28

"There are truths which are not for all men, nor for all times."
—VOLTAIRE

APRIL 9, 1881
LA MESILLA, NEW MEXICO TERRITORY

He clenched both fists until the knuckles whitened, feeling the beginnings of an asthma attack, when William H. Bonney took the stand. Ira Leonard had been unable to deliver a note to Bonney during the noon recess. Sheriff Southwick— most likely bowing to William Rynerson or Bob Olinger—had stationed a deputy outside in front of the barred window. He should have known better, should have known that Albert Fountain and John Bail were first and foremost Masons, then lawyers. They owed their souls to the Santa Fe Ring.

"What is your name and place of residence?"

"William Bonney. My name's William Bonney." His chains jostled as he pointed out the courtroom's main doorway. "I've been living in Sheriff Southwick's calaboose since late last month."

Bristol pounded his gavel. "This is no time for jokes, Bonney."

"Well, then, I've been living in Lincoln, White Oaks, and Fort Sumner. I was living in Lincoln County, at John Tunstall's ranch, when the troubles began." He looked up and smiled at the judge. "How's that?"

Instead of Bail, Fountain was handling the direct examination. "Are you also known as Billy Kid, and Antrim?"

Bonney seemed glad of the chance to correct that point. "Yes, sir, I am. But I was never Billy the Kid, not that I know of. Governor Wallace started calling me that, and the newspaper picked it up, but I was just Billy, Billito, the Kid. I've been called a lot of things."

Fountain shook his head and offered a rare smile. "You take things easy, don't you?"

The witness's grin easily outshone his attorney's. "What's the use of looking on the gloomy side of everything? The laugh's on me this time."

"How do you make your livelihood?"

"I haven't stolen any stock, if that's what you mean. I made my living by gambling, but that was the only way I could live. They wouldn't let me settle down. If they had, I wouldn't be here today." He rattled the chains again. He seemed to enjoy that, seemed to be enjoying himself.

"Who, Billy? Who wouldn't let you live?"

"Jimmy Dolan, Jessie Evans . . ." He turned his head and stared momentarily at Judge Bristol, running his tongue over his protruding teeth, contemplating naming the judge as one of the conspirators, but finally shrugged and faced the jury again. "Men of the House, Dolan's hoodlums, and the Santa Fe Ring."

Newcomb objected. "There is no proof that such a ring exists, Your Honor."

"Sustained."

That was no surprise. The Ring owned Warren Bristol, too.

"Was Sheriff Brady one of those men, Billy?"

"There were certain men who wouldn't let me live in the country. He was one of them."

"But he was a lawman."

"That doesn't mean much in the West, sir. Criminy, Pat Garrett was rustling cows before he became a lawman." Newcomb fired out an objection, but Bonney kept talking, hurrying to finish before Bristol unleashed his gavel on Bonney's head. "I was a lawman before he ever was. Funny how things turned out."

Bonney punctuated his statement with a smirk while Bristol admonished him. "Mister, when there is an objection, you immediately stop speaking until I have made my ruling. You talk out of turn once more, and I will hold you in contempt." He spit tobacco juice and instructed the jury to disregard the witness's statement.

Bonney added: "I don't have problems with Pat, though. He's a good fellow. But Chisum, he got me—"

Bristol's gavel pounded, and Bonney apologized. *His mouth, his cocksure attitude.* Leonard shook his head. He would never have allowed Bonney to testify for those reasons. A few moments passed before Fountain resumed the examination. "It is in your estimation, Mr. Bonney, that Sheriff Brady did not uphold the law of Lincoln County?"

"He upheld it if it suited him. If it suited Lawrence G. Murphy or Jimmy Dolan. When Mr. Tunstall opened his store, the House started losing business, and that was something Dolan could not live with. It wasn't his nature. Then Dolan got into a feud with Mr. McSween, something over some inheritance. Never really understood all of that. So Dolan got Sheriff Brady to hold Mr. Tunstall's property as part of the suit against Mr. McSween, but that wasn't right, not fair. And even before that, Brady had threatened Mr. Tunstall, threatened to kill him, and likely would have if Mr. McSween hadn't stepped between them, if there hadn't been other witnesses."

A chair squeaked as Simon Newcomb rose with another objection. "I don't see how any of this uncorroborated testimony is pertinent to the case at hand."

Fountain was prepared, though. "He opened the door, Your Honor. The prosecutor introduced Tunstall's murder."

"So he did," Bristol said. "But let's speed things up, Mr. Fountain."

"When John Tunstall was murdered—"

"Objection, there—"

Fountain didn't wait. "There are indictments, Your Honor. Indictments handed down by a grand jury that you yourself impaneled. Mr. Tunstall was murdered—"

The gavel popped again. "Let's move on, gentlemen. Mr. Tunstall was shot and killed. There are indictments, but no one had been tried for the crime; therefore, it cannot yet be determined if he was the victim of a crime or was killed, as officers have said, resisting arrest."

When Fountain spoke, the edge in his voice surprised Leonard. Maybe he had underestimated the attorney. "After Mr. Tunstall was found with a bullet in his breast and his face beaten in with the butt of a rifle till his brains poured out, did you try to serve arrest warrants for James Dolan and Jessie Evans?"

So far, Fountain and Bonney had held up pretty good, but Leonard still felt that putting Bonney on the stand was a catastrophe.

"I did." Bonney said. "Brady knocked out the constable, hauled him off to jail with me and Fred Waite, who were assisting him as Regulators, duly appointed by Justice Wilson. He kept us in jail for days, till Mr. McSween made him release us with a court order. And he didn't give us our weapons back, either. He had no call to keep them."

"Others were killed?"

"In Lincoln County in 1878? Yes, sir, you could hardly count that high, seemed like. We feared for our lives, lived in cold camps, hid in caves while trying to round up the men who murdered Mr. Tunstall."

"You caught two of those men, didn't you?"

"Yes, sir. We rode down Morton and Baker, took them to John Chisum's ranch. We were trying to deliver them to Sheriff Brady, though I didn't think it would do much good. Prisoners were always escaping from Brady, if he wanted them to. We were in a canyon after we left the Chisum ranch. William McCloskey, he was a Regulator, had been a friend to Mr. Tunstall, he rode alongside Morton. Morton grabbed Will's six-shooter, shot him in the heart. Then he and Baker made a run for the top of the canyon. Morton fired back at us—we were chasing them by then—and we shot back."

"But you left their bodies where they fell."

Bonney nodded. "If we had delivered them dead to Brady, he would have killed us."

"Billy, why did you go to Lincoln on the day Sheriff Brady was killed?"

"To protect Mr. McSween. He was coming into town that day. We got there the night before, spent the night at the corral at Mr. Tunstall's store. We knew Brady had a warrant for Mr. McSween, and we knew if he ever served it, Mr. McSween would be planted alongside Mr. Tunstall."

"Did you kill the sheriff?"

"No, sir."

"Do you know who did?"

"No, sir."

"But you were in the corral when the Regulators started shooting."

"Yes, sir. We learned from a Mexican boy—I don't want to say his name, because that would mean his death—that Sheriff Brady and a bunch of man-killers planned on ambushing Mr. McSween when he rode into town later that day. Henry Brown started shooting when he saw them, and the others joined in."

"Where were you at this time?"

"Feeding Mr. Tunstall's bulldog."

Fountain paused, swallowed, and gave Bonney an icy stare. "Rob Widenmann said he was feeding the dog."

"He's a liar."

Leonard closed his eyes. Bonney was calling a defense witness a liar.

"And you did not run out to Brady's body?"

"No, sir. I rode out after the shooting."

"Witnesses have identified you."

"They're mistaken. They saw a fellow running in a big Mexican sombrero, but that doesn't mean it was me. By jingo, you could ask Charlie Bowdre or Big Tom that. They'd know I'm telling the truth. Charlie and Tom got killed because a bunch of assassins thought they were aiming at me."

"So you think you are innocent?"

"I know I'm innocent. Besides, I wasn't the only Regulator in Lincoln that day. I think it hard I should be the only one to suffer the extreme penalty of the law."

As Fountain returned to his chair, finished with the examination, William Rynerson stood, excusing himself as he bumped legs, made his way from his bench to the aisle, and left the courtroom. Leonard found that odd, felt tempted to follow him, but had to stay, needed to hear Simon Newcomb's cross.

"Why did you become a Regulator?" the prosecutor asked.

Bonney shrugged. "Seemed like a good idea."

"You were interested in justice?"

"I wanted to bring the men who killed Mr. Tunstall to justice, that's true."

"Perhaps you can explain this loyalty. You knew John Henry Tunstall, a foreigner, for what, six months, maybe? You worked for him. He paid you wages. Yet when he was killed, you felt a strong desire for revenge—a man you hardly knew."

Shaking his head emphatically, Bonney said, "I knew him well. He treated me kindly, gave me a chance when most folks in this territory wouldn't. He didn't deserve to die like that, and those . . . those . . . those vermin who murdered him sure didn't deserve to run about the territory like they were royalty."

Newcomb smiled. "He was . . . how is it you put it, a *pal?*"

"Yeah. He was a pal, not just to me, but to Dick Brewer, Charlie, Big Tom, Frenchy, the McSweens, even that skinflint and hard rock John Chisum."

"And they were your pals, too, especially Bowdre and O'Folliard."

"Good friends, indeed." He nodded his head with enthusiasm. "Had a lot of laughs together. I wish Pat hadn't killed them."

"You respected, admired John Tunstall?"

"Yes, sir."

Newcomb's voice rose as he lashed out his attack. "And you would have these twelve jurors believe that you had nothing to do with the murder of Sheriff Brady! You were feeding your employer's *dog!* Isn't it the truth, sir, that you orchestrated this whole act? You rode to Lincoln, knocked holes in the corral wall for your rifles, waited for Sheriff Brady to walk by so you could murder him. That's the truth of the matter, isn't it? This was an act of revenge, a willful and felonious act of premeditated murder."

Bonney remained calm. "If it was anything, sir, it was self-defense."

Newcomb stared at the jury as he spoke. "Self-defense. And Morton and Baker were killed trying to escape." His laugh lacked humor. "Isn't it true, sir, that you rushed out of the corral and ran toward the lifeless, blood-soaked body of Sheriff Brady to steal the warrants he possessed, that alias warrant you have mentioned for Alexander McSween?"

Now Bonney laughed. "What good would that have done, counselor? You should know better. You think I would risk my life for a piece of paper? Criminy, the judge here would have just wrote out another one."

Rynerson had made his way back into the courtroom. He nodded at Newcomb but didn't bother returning to his seat. Instead, after the prosecutor acknowledged Rynerson's gesture, the towering former district attorney left again. *What are they up to?* Leonard wondered.

"Your character witnesses say you are a good man, a man who looks after his friends. Do you agree with their assessment?"

"I'm not one to judge."

"But you value friendship. That's why you joined the Regulators, isn't it?"

"A man's not much if he doesn't . . . " Bonney stopped, his boyish expression vanishing, as if some memory had reached up and gripped a stranglehold over his throat. He stared blankly, finally shuddered and shook his head, his manacles shaking as he sank back in his chair. "I try to look after my pals. I tried to look after Mr. Tunstall, but Jessie Evans and the Ring murdered him. I tried to take care of Mr. McSween, but they killed him, too. And I reckon they're bound and determined to send me chasing after them." He sat up, defiant again. "Let them try."

Newcomb was in his chair before Bonney had finished.

"Any more questions?" Bristol asked.

"No, Your Honor," Newcomb said. "I cannot get a straight answer from the defendant, so I am finished with him."

A moment later, the defense rested its case.

CHAPTER 30

"Murder in the first degree is the greatest crime known to our laws. The legislature of this territory has enacted a law prescribing that the punishment for murder in the first degree shall be death. This is the law: no other punishment than death can be imposed for murder in the first degree."

—JUDGE WARREN BRISTOL

APRIL 9, 1881
LA MESILLA, NEW MEXICO TERRITORY

In his chambers, Warren Bristol poured four fingers of Tennessee whiskey into his glass, settled into his chair, and began reading the instructions to the jury Albert Fountain had requested.

1. Under the evidence, the jury must either find the defendant guilty of murder in the first degree or acquit him.

2. The jury will not be justified in finding the defendant guilty of murder in the first degree unless they are satisfied from the evidence, to the exclusion of all reasonable doubt, that the defendant actually fired the shot that caused the death of the deceased Brady, and that such a shot was fired by the defendant—with a premeditated design to effect the death of the deceased, or that the defendant was present and actually assisted in firing the fatal shot or shots that caused the death of the deceased, and that he was in a position to render such assistance and actually present and rendered such assistance from a premeditated design to effect the death of the deceased.

And so forth.

He skipped over the third and fourth instructions, saw where John Bail had signed his name underneath Fountain's, and tossed the paper onto his desk. Bail might have put his signature on the request, but it had been written entirely by Fountain. Bristol finished his drink and thought about having another, but it wouldn't do for the presiding judge to have whiskey on his breath when he instructed the jury.

Fountain was a pretty good attorney, had fought hard, but he never should have let Bonney take the stand. Bristol had John Bail to thank for that. He opened a new plug of tobacco and bit off a sizable chaw, worked it until it was soft, then picked up a pencil and began writing his own instructions. He had two hours to finish. That's how long he had called the recess.

"Gentlemen of the jury," Bristol began, blocking out the interpreter's Spanish translation, "the defendant in this case, William Bonney, alias Kid, alias William Antrim, is charged in and by the indictment against him . . . "

He wondered if those twelve Mexicans could understand this legal babbling, wondered if even Mariano Toribio knew what he was really saying. He reminded those dumb greasers that Bonney was charged with the murder of Sheriff William Brady, that they were hearing the case here in Old Mesilla because of a change of venue from Lincoln County.

"In the matter of determining what your verdict shall be, it would be improper for you to consider anything except that evidence before you," Bristol said. "You as jurors are the exclusive judges of the weight of the evidence." *Make them feel proud.* "You are the exclusive judges of the credibility of the witnesses. It is for you to determine whether the testimony of any witness whom you have heard is to be believed or not." *Remind them that the Kid is a liar.* "You are also the exclusive judges whether the evidence is sufficiently clear and strong to satisfy your minds that the defendant is guilty." *You know damned well he's guilty, and if you don't, savvy this:*

"There is no evidence tending to show that the killing of Brady was either justifiable or excusable. As a matter of law, therefore, such killing was unlawful, and whoever committed the deed or was present and advised, aided or abetted, or consented to such killing committed the crime of murder in some one of the degrees of murder.

"There is no evidence before you showing that the killing of Brady is murder in any other degree than the first." He looked up from his papers briefly. Simon Newcomb tried to hide his smirk, Fountain frowned, Bail just sat there nodding, and the Kid picked at a fingernail with his thumbnail.

"Your verdict therefore should be either that the defendant is guilty of murder in the first degree or that he is not guilty at all under this indictment."

He explained murder and the law to the jurors. Finally, he got to the main instructions.

"In this case, in order to justify you in finding this defendant guilty of murder in the first degree under the particular circumstances as presented by the indictment and the evidence, you should be satisfied and believe from the evidence to the exclusion of every reasonable doubt of the truth of several propositions:

"First. That the defendant either inflicted one or more of the fatal wounds causing Brady's death, or that he was present at the time and place of the killing, and encouraged, incited, aided in, abetted, advised, or commanded such killing.

"Second. That such killing was without justification or excuse.

"Third. That such killing was caused by inflicting upon Brady's body a fatal gunshot wound.

"And fourth. That such fatal wound was either inflicted by the defendant from a premeditated design to effect Brady's death, or that he was present at the time and place of the killing of Brady, and from a premeditated design to effect his death, he then and there encouraged, incited, aided in, abetted, advised, or commanded such killing.

"If he was present—encouraging, inciting, aiding in, abetting, advising, or commanding this killing of Brady—he is as much guilty as though he fired the fatal shot. This is the law of the land."

He had to go on, defining "reasonable doubt" as he did in all criminal cases, but he felt confident that even a bunch of illiterate greasers would have no choice but to bring in a verdict of guilty. Albert Fountain had delivered a fine closing argument, but Simon Newcomb's rebuttal had also been solid. Bristol finished, listening to Toribio's translation and scowling at the jury. *Make them fear me, so they won't bring in the wrong verdict.*

As the bailiff led them away to deliberate, Bristol pulled out his pocket watch. He would give them ten minutes to reach a verdict.

They came back in seven.

APRIL 11, 1881
LA MESILLA, NEW MEXICO TERRITORY

"Hello, Billy."

The Kid opened his eyes and faked a yawn. He swung his legs over the bunk, sat up, then shook his head as if his visitor had woken him up. Hell, a body couldn't catch a wink of sleep with all the noise going on outside.

"I reckon I shouldn't have testified," he said with a grin, "eh, Ira?"

Leonard didn't smile. His hair looked even whiter than it had been before the trial began, and he held a rolled-up copy of *Newman's Semi-Weekly* in his left hand, clenching it hard. The Kid had already read the editor's assault on William H. Bonney's good name. "Where you been keeping yourself?"

"I was at the trial," Leonard said. "I tried to get inside, but they weren't letting you have any visitors; at least, they weren't letting me see you. I told you the chances were good we would lose on this level, Billy. I don't want you worrying. I can handle your appeal."

With a chuckle, the Kid stood, but instead of walking toward Leonard, he jumped, grabbing the window's iron bars, and pulled himself up to stare at the crowd outside the Corn Exchange Hotel. "I think I'm gonna stick with Mr. Fountain, Ira. He said he'd represent me on appeal if I can get him some money. I'm trying to get my bay horse back. One of those damned brigands with Garrett stole it back at Stinking Springs."

His back to Leonard, the Kid smiled when Leonard mumbled an *Oh, I see.* He expected Leonard to leave, but the attorney stayed in the hallway, talking about legal affairs until the Kid's arms tired and he dropped to the floor.

"The testimony of Billie Wilson should be grounds for appeal," Leonard was saying. "I can also argue that Judge Bristol should have stepped down. The rumor in Lincoln County back in '78 was that you wanted him dead, so he couldn't be impartial. And with his instructions, the jury had no choice but to find you guilty."

Shaking his head, the Kid told Leonard to shut up. Leonard looked up, his mouth agape, as the Kid faced him.

"Ira, I *am* guilty. Criminy, you know that. I killed Brady, and I helped kill Hindman. I'm a better sharpshooter than any of those with me, including Henry Brown. You think I missed? Every bullet I fired found its mark. It was me who ran to Brady's body, not to grab some stupid warrant, but to get my rifle back. Brady stole it from me, that spud-eating bastard. I can show you the scar in my thigh where Billy Mathews almost shot my pecker off."

Suddenly tired, he sat down. "I don't have any regrets, either. Except that I got caught, tried, and convicted when Henry and the others lit a shuck for parts unknown. Brady, Dolan, Evans . . . those men killed John Tunstall, killed a lot of good men, but that's the law for you. . . . The law of the land, at least *this* land." He pointed his chin at the empty cell behind Leonard. Billie Wilson had been shipped off to Santa Fe immediately after the trial. "Hell, I don't even blame Billie for what he did, that little *hijo de carbón*."

He shook his head and stared at his manacled feet. "You and Albert are wasting your time. I don't think I'll make it to Lincoln. Bob Olinger is looking for a reason to kill me. Likely, I'll be dead before we get out to Pat Coghlan's ranch."

Leonard cleared his throat. "I'll pray for you, Billy."

That prompted another laugh. "Funny how things change, Ira. It's like I said the other day. Pat Garrett was a bandit before he was a lawman, and I was a lawman before they called me a bandit. You were one of the biggest sinners I know."

"I'll be in Lincoln, Billy. I will—"

"I am what I am of choice," the Kid said firmly, and sighed. "It'll be over shortly."

Leonard fell silent. The Kid leaned back in his bunk, pulled a hat over his eyes, and listened to Leonard's footsteps growing fainter down the hall.

APRIL 13, 1881
LA MESILLA, NEW MEXICO TERRITORY

When Bristol asked if he had anything to say before passing sentence, the Kid just shook his head. He sat beside his attorneys, with Bob Olinger standing behind him, shotgun in hand. They must have thought him to be one bad *hombre* since he had just been found guilty of first-degree murder.

"Very well," Bristol said solemnly. "It is therefore considered by the court here that the said defendant, William Bonney, alias Kid, alias William Antrim, be taken to the County of Lincoln, in the Third Judicial District of the Territory of New Mexico, by the sheriff of Doña Ana County in said judicial district and territory and there by him delivered into the custody of the sheriff of the said County of Lincoln, and that he, the said William Bonney, alias Kid, alias William Antrim, be confined in prison in said County of Lincoln by the sheriff of such county until Friday, the thirteenth day of May, in the year of our Lord One Thousand Eight Hundred and Eight-one. That on the day aforesaid, between the hours of nine of the clock in the forenoon and three of the clock in the afternoon, he, the said William Bonney, alias Kid, alias William Antrim, be taken from such prison to some suitable and convenient place of execution within said County of Lincoln, by the sheriff of said county, and that then and there on that day and between the aforesaid hours thereof, by the sheriff of said County of

Lincoln, he, the said William Bonney, alias Kid, alias William Antrim, be hanged by the neck until his body be dead."

The shotgun pressed against the Kid's spine. "All that legal talk, my boy, means you're a dead man," Olinger said in a hoarse whisper.

The Kid bit his lip to keep from smiling. They were going to hang him on *Friday the Thirteenth?*

CORRESPONDENCE WITH GOVERNOR LEW WALLACE

The correspondence between Billy the Kid and Territorial Governer Lew Wallace span the period from March 1879 until March 1881 and show the changing relationship between the two. In the early letters, Billy is confident and Wallace is responsive to him. In the later letters we see Billy becoming increasingly desperate as he faces the hangman's noose. He pleads in vain for Wallace to intervene.

CORRESPONDENCE WITH GOVERNOR LEW WALLACE

Lincoln, March 15, 1879

W.H. Bonney,

Come to the house of old Squire Wilson (not the lawyer) at nine (9) o'clock next Monday night alone. I don't mean his office, but his residence. Follow along the foot of the mountain south of the town, come in on that side, and knock at the east door. I have authority to exempt you from prosecution, if you will testify to what you say you know.

The object of the meeting at Squire Wilson's is to arrange the matter in a way to make your life safe. To do that the utmost secrecy is to be used. So come alone. Don't tell anybody—not a living soul—where you are coming or the object. If you could trust Jesse Evans, you can trust me.

Lew Wallace.

—

San Patricio

Lincoln County

Thursday [March] 20th 1879

General Lew. Wallace:

Sir, I will keep the appointment I made but be Sure and have men come that You can depend on I am not afraid to die like a man fighting but I would not like to be killed like a dog unarmed. tell Kimbal to let his men be placed around the house. and for him to come in alone; and he can arrest us.

all I am afraid of is that in the Fort we might be poisioned, or killed through a Window at night. but you can arrange that all right. tell the Commanding Officer to watch Lt. Goodwin (he would not hesitate to do anything) there will be danger on the road of Somebody waylaying us to kill us on the road to the Fort. You will never catch those fellows on the road. Watch Fritzes, Captain Bacas ranch and the Brewery they will either go to Seven Rivers or to Picarillo Montians they will stay around close untilll the scouting parties come in. give a Spy a pair of glasses and let him get on the mountain back of Fritzes and watch and if they are there ther will be provisons carried to them. it is not my place to advise you, but I am anxious to have them caught, and perhaps know how men hide from Soldiers better than you. please excuse me for having so much to Say and I still remain Yours Truly
W H. Bonney
P.S.
I have changed my mind Send Kimbal to Gutieres just below San Patricio one mile because Sanger and Ballard are or were great friends of Caniels Ballard told me [crossed out text: today] yesterday to leave for you were doing everything to catch me. it was a blind to get me to leave tell Kimbal not to come before 8 oclock for I may not be there before

—

Fort Stanton, March 20, 1879
W. H. Bonney
The escape makes no difference in arrangements. [crossed out text: I will comply with my part, if you will with yours.]

To remove all suspicion of [crossed out text: arrangement] understanding, I think it better to put the arresting party in charge of Sheriff Kimball, who will be instructed to see that no violence is used. This will go to you tonight. [crossed out text: If you still insist upon Hudgins, let me know.] If I don't get [crossed out text: receive] other word from you, the party (all citizens) will be at the junction by 3 o'clock tomorrow
Lew Wallace

—

Fort Sumner
Dec 12th 1880
Gov. Lew Wallace
Dear Sir
I noticed in the Las Vegas Gazette a piece which stated that, Billy the Kid, the name of which I am known in the Country was the Captain of a Band of Outlaws who hold Forth at the Portales. There is no such organization in Existence. So the Gentleman must have Drawn very heavily on his Imagination. My business at the White Oaks the time I was waylaid and my horse Killed was to see Judge Leonard who has my case in hand. he had written to me to come up, that he thought he could get Everything Straighened up. I did not find him at the Oaks & Should have gone to Lincoln if I had met with no accident. After mine and Billie Wilsons horses were killed we both made our way to a Station forty miles from the Oaks kept by Mr. Greathouse. When I got up next morning The house was Surrounded by an outfit led by one Carlyle, Who came into the house and demanded a Surrender. I asked for their Papers

and they had none. So I Concluded it amounted to nothing more than a mob and told Carlyle that he would have to Stay in the house and lead the way out that night. Soon after a note was brought in Stating that if Carlyle did not come out inside of five minutes they would kill the Station Keeper Greathouse who had left the house and was with them. in a Short time a shot was fired on the outside and Carlyle thinking Greathouse was Killed jumped through the window breaking the Sash as he went and was killed by his own Party they thinking it was me trying to make my Escape. the party then withdrew. they returned the next day and burned an old man named Spencer's house and Greathouses also I made my way to this Place afoot and During my absence Deputy Sheriff Garrett Acting under Chisums orders went to the Portalio and found Nothing. on his way back he went by Mr. Yerbys ranch and took a pair of mules of mine which I had left with Mr Bowdre who is in charge of Mr Yerbys cattle. he (Garrett) claimed that they were stolen and Even if they were not he had a right to Confiscate any outlaws property I have been at Sumner Since I left Lincoln making my living Gambling the mules were bought by me the truth of which I can prove by the best citizens around Sumner. J.S. Chisum is the man who got me into Trouble and was benefited Thousands by it and is now doing all he can against me. There is no Doubt but what there is a great deal of Stealing going on in the Territory and a great deal of the Property is taken across the Plains as it is a good outlet but so far as my being at the head of a Band there is nothing of it in several Instances I have recovered Stolen Property where there was no chance to get an Officer to do it. One Instance for Hugo Zuber Postoffice Puerto De Luna. another for Pablo Analla Same Place. If some impartial Party were to investigate this matter they would find it far Different from the impression put out by Chisum and his Tools.

Yours Respect

William Bonney

—

Santa Fe

Jan. 1st

1881

Gov. Lew Wallace

Dear Sir

I would like to See you for a few moments if you can spare time

Yours Respect.

W. H. Bonney

—

Santa Fe in jail

March 4th 1881

Gov. Lew Wallace

Dear Sir

I wrote you a little note the day before yesterday, but have received no answer. I Expect you have forgotten what you promised me, this month two Years ago. but I have not, and I think You had ought to have come and seen me as I requested you to. I have done Everything that I promised you I would, and you have done nothing that you promised me. I think

when you think the matter over, you will come down and See me, and I can then Explain Everything to you. Judge Leonard Passed through here on his way East in January and promised to come and see me on his way back but he did not fulfill his Promise. it looks to me like I am getting left in the Cold. I am not treated right by Sherman. he lets Every Stranger that comes to See me through Curiosity in to See me, but will not let a single one of my friends in, not Even an Attorney. I guess they mean to Send me up without giving me any show. but they will have a nice time doing it I am not ntirely without friends I shall Expect to see you Sometime today
Patiently Waiting
I am Very Truly Yours Respect
Wm. H. Bonney

—

Santa Fe New Mexico
March 27/81
Gov Lew Wallace
Dear Sir
for the last time I ask, Will you Keep your promise. I start below tomorrow Send answer by bearer
Yours Respt
W Bonney

PAT F. GARRETT

THE AUTHENTIC LIFE OF BILLY, THE KID

In this excerpt from his personal, albeit largely ghostwritten account, Pat Garrett tells us how and why he killed Billy the Kid, including a description of the events leading up to the deed. It seemed incredible to him that Billy the Kid would linger so long in the territory—but linger he did. Garrett tells us how he found him and of his own trepidation at the thought of having to face such a dangerous young man. When finally located, Billy the Kid failed to fire first and ask questions later. He asked "Quien es?" ("Who is it?") and Garrett responded with two shots.

Garrett was a long-time rancher and lawman in New Mexico and Texas, and was rumored to have been an occasional horse thief. He enlisted a newspaperman, Ash Upson, to help him write his book.

EXCERPTS FROM
THE AUTHENTIC LIFE OF BILLY, THE KID

By Pat Garrett
1927

CHAPTER XXIII
AGAIN ON THE TRAIL—THE KID HUNTED DOWN—THE FATAL
SHOT IN THE DARK—THE KID DIES, BUT NOT WITH HIS BOOTS ON

——————◦•◉•◦——————

During the weeks following the Kid's escape, I was censured by some for my seeming unconcern and inactivity in the matter of his re-arrest. I was egotistical enough to think I knew my own business best, and preferred to accomplish this duty, if possible at all, in my own way. I was constantly, but quietly, at work, seeking sure information and maturing my plans of action. I did not lay about the Kid's old haunts, nor disclose my intentions and operations to any one. I stayed at home, most of the time, and busied myself about the ranch. If my seeming unconcern deceived the people and gave the Kid confidence in his security, my end was accomplished. It was my belief that the Kid was still in the country and haunted the vicinity of Fort Sumner; yet there was some doubt mingled with my belief. He was never taken for a fool, but was credited with the possession of extraordinary forethought and cool judgment, for one of his age. It seemed incredible that, in his situation, with the extreme penalty of law, the reward of detection, and the way of successful flight and safety open to him—with no known tie to bind him to that dangerous locality—it seemed incredible that he should linger in the Territory. My first task was to solve my doubts.

Early in July, I received a reply from a letter I had written to Mr. Brazil. I was at Lincoln when this letter came to me. Mr. Brazil was dodging and hiding from the Kid. He feared his vengeance on account of the part which he, Brazil, had taken in his capture. There were many others who "trembled in their boots" at the knowledge of his escape; but most of them talked him out of his resentment, or conciliated him in some manner.

Brazil's letter gave me no positive information. He said he had not seen the Kid since his escape, but, from many indications, believed he was still in the country. He offered me any assistance in his power to recapture him. I again wrote to Brazil, requesting him to meet me at the mouth of Tayban Arroyo an hour after dark on the night of the 13th day of July.

A gentleman named John W. Poe, who had superceded Frank Stewart, in the employ of the stockmen of the Canadian, was at Lincoln on business, as was one of my deputies, Thomas K. McKinney. I first went to McKinney, and told him I wanted him to accompany me on a business trip to Arizona, that we would go down home and start from there. He consented. I then went to Poe and to him I disclosed my business and all its particulars, showing him my correspondence. He also complied with my request that he should accompany me.

We three went to Roswell and started up the Rio Pecos from there on the night of July 10th. We rode mostly in the night, followed no roads, but taking unfrequented routes, and arrived at the mouth of Tayban Arroyo, five miles south of Fort Sumner one hour after dark on the night of July 13th. Brazil was not there. We waited nearly two hours, but he did not come. We rode off a mile or two, staked our horses, and slept until daylight. Early in the morning we rode up into the hills and prospected awhile with our field glasses.

Poe was a stranger in the county and there was little danger that he would meet any one who knew him at Sumner. So, after an hour or two spent in the hills, he went into Sumner to take observations. I advised him, also, to go on to Sunnyside, seven miles above Sumner, and interview M. Rudolph, Esq., in whose judgment and discretion I had great confidence. I arranged with Poe to meet us that night at moonrise, at La Punta de la Glorietta, four miles north of Fort Sumner. Poe went on to the plaza, and McKinney and myself rode down into the Pecos Valley, where we remained during the day. At night we started our circling around the town and met Poe exactly on time at the trysting place.

Poe's appearance at Sumner had excited no particular observation, and he had gleaned no news there. Rudolph thought, from all indications, that the Kid was about; and yet, at times, he doubted. His cause for doubt seemed to be based on no evidence except the fact that the Kid was no fool, and no man in his sense, under the circumstances, would brave such danger.

I then concluded to go and have a talk with Peter Maxwell, Esq., in whom I felt sure I could rely. We had ridden to within a short distance of Maxwell's grounds when we found a man in camp and stopped. To Poe's great surprise, he recognized in the camper an old friend and former partner, in Texas, named Jacobs. We unsaddled here, got some coffee, and, on foot, entered an orchard which runs from this point down to a row of old buildings, some of them occupied by Mexicans, not more than sixty yards from Maxwell's house. We approached these houses cautiously, and when within ear shot, heard the sound of voices conversing in Spanish. We concealed ourselves quickly and listened; but the distance was too great to hear words, or even distinguish voices. Soon a man arose from the ground, in full view, but too far away to recognize. He wore a broad-brimmed hat, a dark vest and pants, and was in his shirt sleeves. With a few words, which fell like a murmur on our ears, he went to the fence, jumped it, and walked down towards Maxwell's house.

Little as we then suspected it, this man was the Kid. We learned, subsequently, that, when he left his companions that night, he went to the house of a Mexican friend, pulled off his hat and boots, threw himself on a bed, and commenced reading a newspaper. He soon, however, hailed his friend, who was sleeping in the room, told him to get up and make some coffee, adding:—"Give me a butcher knife and I will go over to Pete's and get some beef; I'm hungry." The Mexican arose, handed him the knife, and the Kid, hatless and in his stocking-feet, started to Maxwell['s], which was but a few steps distant.

When the Kid, by me unrecognized, left the orchard, I motioned to my companions, and we cautiously retreated a short distance, and, to avoid the persons whom we had heard at the houses, took another route, approaching Maxwell's house from the opposite direction. When we reached the porch in front of the building, I left Poe and McKinney at the end of the porch, about twenty feet from the door of Pete's room, and went in. It was near midnight and Pete was in bed. I walked to the head of the bed and sat down on it, beside him, near the pillow. I asked him as to the whereabouts of the Kid. He said that the Kid had certainly been about, but he did not know whether he had left or not. At that moment a man sprang quickly into the door, looking back, and called twice in Spanish, "Who comes there?" No one replied and he came on in. He was bareheaded. From his step I could perceive he was either barefooted or in his stocking-feet, and held a revolver in his right hand and a butcher knife in his left.

He came directly towards me. Before he reached the bed, I whispered: "Who is it, Pete?" but received no reply for a moment. It struck me that it might be Pete's brother-in-law, Manuel Abreu, who had seen Poe and McKinney, and wanted to know their business. The intruder came close to me, leaned both hands on the bed, his right hand almost touching my knee, and asked, in a low tone:—Who are they Pete?"— at the same instant Maxwell whispered to me. "That's him!" Simultaneously the Kid must have seen, or felt, the presence of a third person at the head of the bed. He raised quickly his pistol, a self cocker, within a foot of my breast. Retreating rapidly across the room he cried: "*Quien es? Quien es?*" ("Who's that? Who's that?") All this occurred in a moment. Quickly as possible I drew my revolver and fired, threw my body aside, and fired again. The second shot was useless; the Kid fell dead. He never spoke. A struggle or two, a little strangling sound as he gasped for breath, and the Kid was with his many victims.

Maxwell had plunged over the foot of the bed on the floor, dragging the bed-clothes with him. I went to the door and met Poe and McKinney there. Maxwell rushed past me, out on the porch; they threw their guns down on him, when he cried: "Don't shot, don't shoot." I told my companions I had got the Kid. They asked me if I had not shot the wrong man. I told them I had made no blunder, that I knew the Kid's voice too well to be mistaken. The Kid was entirely unknown to either of them. They had seen him pass in, and, as he stepped on the porch, McKinney, who was sitting, rose to his feet; one of his spurs caught under the boards, and nearly threw him. The Kid laughed, but probably, saw their guns, as he drew his revolver and sprang into the doorway, as he hailed: "Who comes there?" Seeing a bareheaded, barefooted man, in his shirt-sleeves, with a butcher knife in his hand, and hearing his hail in excellent Spanish, they naturally supposed him to be a Mexican and an attaché of the establishment, hence their suspicion that I had shot the wrong man.

We now entered the room and examined the body. The ball struck him just above the heart, and must have cut through the ventricles. Poe asked me how many shots I fired; I told him two, but that I had no idea where the second one went. Both Poe and McKinney said the Kid must have fired then, as there were surely three shots fired. I told them that he had fired one shot, between my two. Maxwell said that the Kid fired; yet, when we came to look for bullet marks, none from his pistol could be found. We searched long and faithfully—found both my bullet marks and none other; so, against the impression and senses of four men, we had to conclude that the Kid did not fire at all. We examined his pistol—a self-cocker, caliber 41. It had five cartridges and one shell in the chambers, the hammer resting on the shell, but this proves nothing, as many carry their revolvers in this way for safety; besides, this shell looked as though it had been shot some time before.

It will never be known whether the Kid recognized me or not. If he did, it was the first time, during all his life of peril, that he ever lost his presence of mind, or failed to shoot first and hesitate afterwards. He knew that a meeting with me meant surrender or fight. He told several persons about Sumner that he bore no animosity against me, and had no desire to do me injury. He also said that he knew, should we meet, he would have to surrender, kill me, or get killed himself. So, he declared his intention, should we meet, to commence shooting on sight.

On the following morning, the alcalde, Alejandro Segura, held an inquest on the body. Hon. M. Rudolph, of Sunnyside, was foreman of the coroner's jury. They found a verdict that William H. Bonney came to his death from a gun-shot wound, the weapon in the hands of Pat F. Garrett, that the fatal wound was inflicted by the said Garrett in the discharge of his official duty as sheriff, and that the homicide was justifiable.

The body was neatly and properly dressed and buried in the military cemetery at Fort Sumner, July 15, 1881. His exact age, on the day of his death, was 21 years, 7 months, and 21 days.

I said that the body was buried in the cemetery at Fort Sumner. I wish to add that it is there to-day intact. Skull, fingers, toes, bones, and every hair of the head that was buried with the body on that 15th day of July, doctors, newspaper editors, and paragraphers to the contrary notwithstanding. Some presuming swindlers have claimed to have the Kid's skull on exhibition, or one of his fingers, or some other portion of his body, and one medical gentleman has persuaded credulous idiots that he has all the bones strung upon wires. It is possible that there is a skeleton on exhibition somewhere in the States, or even in this Territory, which was procured somewhere down the Rio Pecos. We have them, lots of them in this section. The banks of the Pecos are dotted from Fort Sumner to the Rio Grande with unmarked graves, and the skeletons are of all sizes, ages, and complexions. Any showman of ghastly curiosities can resurrect one or all of them, and place them on exhibition as the remains of Dick Turpin, Jack Shepherd, Cartouche, or the Kid, with no one to say him nay; so they don't ask the people of the Rio Pecos to believe it.

Again I say that the Kid's body lies undisturbed in the grave—and I speak of what I know.

ADDENDA

The life of the Kid is ended, and my history thereof is finished. Perhaps, however, some of my readers will consent to follow me through three or four additional pages, which may be unnecessary and superfluous, but which I insert for my own personal gratification, and which I invite my friends to read.

During the time occupied in preparing the foregoing work for press, some circumstances have occurred, some newspaper articles have appeared, and many remarks have been passed, referring to the disposal of the Kid, his character, disposition, and history, and my contemplated publication of his life, which I have resolved to notice, against the advice of friends, who believe the proper and more dignified plan would be to ignore them altogether. But I have something to say, and propose to say it.

A San Francisco daily, in an article which I have never seen, but only comments thereon in other journals, among other strictures on my actions, questions my immunity from legal penalty for the slaying of the Kid. I did think I was fully advised in regard to this matter before I undertook the dangerous task of his re-arrest, as I contemplated the possible necessity of having to kill him. But I must acknowledge that I did not consult with the San Francisco editor, and can, at this late hour, only apologize, humbly, for the culpable omission. The law decided as to my amenability to its requirements—should the opinion of the scribbler be adverse, I can but abjectly crave his mercy.

I have been portrayed in print and in illustrations as shooting the Kid from behind a bed, from under a bed, and from other places of concealment. After mature deliberation I have resolved that honest confession will serve my purpose better than prevarication. Hear!

I was not behind the bed, because, in the first place, I could not get there. I'm not "as wide as a church door," but the bed was so close to the wall that a lath could scarce have been introduced between. I was not under the bed, and this fact will require a little more complicated explanation. I *could* have gotten under the bed; but, you see, I did not know the Kid was coming. He took me by surprise—gave me no chance on earth to hide myself. Had I but suspected his proximity, or that he would come upon me in that abrupt manner, I would have utilized any safe place of concealment which might have presented itself—under the bed, or under any article which I might have found under the bed, large enough to cover me.

Scared? Suppose a man of the Kid's noted gentle and amiable disposition and temper had warned you that when you two met you had better "come a shooting"; suppose he bounced in on you unexpectedly with a revolver in his hand, whilst yours was in your scabbard. Scared? Wouldn't you have been scared? I didn't dare to answer his hail:—"*Quien es?*" as the first sound of my voice (which he knew perfectly well), would have been his signal to make a target of my physical personality, with his self-cocker, from which he was wont to pump a continuous stream of fire and lead, and in any direction, unerringly, which answered to his will. Scared, Cap? Well, I should say so. I started out on that expedition with the expectation of getting scared. I went out contemplating the probability of being shot at, and the possibility of being hurt, perhaps killed; but not if any precaution on my part would prevent such a catastrophe. The Kid got a very much better show than I had intended to give him.

Then, "the lucky shot," as they put it. It was not the shot, but the opportunity that was lucky, and everybody may rest assured I did not hesitate long to improve it. If there is any one simple enough to imagine that I did, or will ever, put my life squarely in the balance against that of the Kid, or any of his ilk, let him divest his mind of that absurd fallacy. It is said that Garrett did not give the Kid a fair show—did not fight him "on the square," etc. Whenever I take a contract to fight a man "on the square," as they put it (*par* parenthesis—I am not on the fight), that man must bear the reputation, before the world and in my estimation, of an honorable man and respectable citizen; or, at least, he must be my equal in social standing, and I claim the right to place my own estimate upon my own character, and my own evaluation upon my own life. If the public shall judge that these shall be measured by the same standard as those of outlaws and murderers, whose lives are forfeit to the law, I beg the privilege of appeal from its decision.

I had a hope—a very faint hope—of catching the Kid napping, as it were, so that I might disarm and capture him. Failing in that, my design was to try and get "the drop" on him, with the, almost, certainty, as I believed, that he would make good his threat to "die fighting with a revolver at each ear"; so with the drop, I would have been forced to kill him anyhow. I, at no time, contemplated taking any chances which I could avoid by caution or cunning. The only circumstances under which we could have met on equal terms, would have been accidental, and to which I would have been an unwilling party. Had we met unexpectedly, face to face, I have no idea that either one of us would have run away, and there is where the "square fight" would, doubtless, have come off. With one question I will dismiss the subject of taking unfair advantage, etc. What sort of "square fight," or "even show," would I have got, had one of the Kid's friends in Fort Sumner chanced to see me and informed him of my presence there and at Pete Maxwell's room on the fatal night?

A few words in regard to criticisms from two isolated rural journals published, I think, somewhere in the hilltops of the extreme northern counties of this Territory—at Guadalupitas, or Las Golondrinas, or La Cueva, or Vermejo. I have never seen a copy of either of them, and should have been ignorant of their existence had not a respectable newspaper copied their "puffs." These fellows objected to my writing and publishing a life of the Kid. Their expostulations come too late; it is written and I will quarrel before I abandon the design of publishing it.

One of these weekly emanations is called "The Optician," or some similar name, which would indicate that it is devoted to the interests of an industry which is, or should be, the exclusive prerogative of the disciples of Paul Pry. Perhaps it is a medical journal, edited by an M. D. who did not get the skull, nor the finger, nor any of the bones of the Kid's body, and is proportionately incensed thereat.

The other, judging from the two or three extracts I have seen from its columns, must, also, be a medical journal, published in the interests of an asylum for the imbeciles. I would advise the manager to exercise more vigilance in the absence of the editor and try to keep patients out of his chair. The unfortunate moonling who scribbled that "stickfull" which reflected upon me and my book, judging from his peculiar phraseology, must be a demented fishmonger.

> *You may spatter, you may soak him*
> *With ink if you will,*
> *But the scent of stale cat-fish*
> *Will cling 'round him still.*

Both of these delectable hermits charge me with intent to publish a life of the Kid, with the nefarious object of making money thereby. O! asinine propellers of Faber's No. 2; O! ludificatory lavishers of Arnold's night-tinted fluid; what the Hades else do you suppose my object could be? Their philosophy is that I must not attempt to make any more money out of the result of my "lucky shot," because, forsooth, "some men would have been satisfied," etc. Anybody, everybody else, authors who never were in New Mexico and never saw the Kid, can compile from newspaper rumors, as many lives of him as they please, make all the money out of their bogus, unreliable heroics that can be extorted from a gullible public, and these fellows will congratulate them; but my truthful history should be suppressed, because I got paid for ridding the country of a criminal. How do these impertinent intermeddlers know how much money I have made by this accident, or incident, or by whatever name they choose to designate it? How do they know how many thousands of dollars worth of stock and other property I have saved to those who "rewarded" me, by the achievement? Whose business is it if I choose to publish a hundred books, and make money out of them all, though I were as rich as the Harper Brothers? Wonder if either of these discontented fellows would have refused to publish my book on shares. Wonder what would have been the color of their notices, and when they would have "been satisfied." It's bile, Cully! nothing but bile. Take Indian Root Pills. And yet I thank you for your unsolicited, gratuitous notices, valueless as they are. They may help to sell a few copies of my work in your secluded locality. But, as I am no subject for charity (though your articles would seem to say so), send in reasonable bills and I will pay them. I know the difficulties under which projectors of newspapers in isolated regions labor, and would have sent you each a liberal advertisement *without a hint,* had I known of your existence.

It is amusing to notice how brave some of the Kid's "ancient enemies," and, even, some who professed to be his friends, have become since there is no danger of their courage being put to test by an interview with him. Some of them say that the Kid was a coward (which is a cowardly lie), and anybody, with any nerve, could have arrested him without trouble, thus obviating the necessity of killing him. One has seen him slapped in the face when he had a revolver in his hand, and he did not resent it. One has seen a Mexican, over on the Rio Grande, choke him against the wall, the Kid crying and begging with a cocked pistol in his hand. These blowers are unworthy of notice. Most of them were vagabonds who had "slopped" over from one faction to the other during the war, regulating their maneuvers according to the prospect of danger or safety, always keeping in view their chances to steal a sore-back pony or a speckled calf, and aspiring to the appellation of stock-owners. There is not one of these brave mouth-fighters that would have dared to give voice to such lying bravado whilst the Kid lived, though he were chained in a cell; not one of them that, were he on their track, would not have set the prairie on fire to get out of his reach, and, in their fright, extinguished it again as they ran, leaving a wet trail behind. These silly vaporings are but repeated illustrations of that old fable, "The Dead Lion and the Live Ass."

I will now take leave of all those of my readers who have not already taken "French leave" of me. Whatever may be the cause of the effect, Lincoln County now enjoys a season of peace and prosperity to which she has ever, heretofore, been a stranger. No Indians, no desperadoes, to scare our citizens from their labors, or disturb their slumbers. Stock wanders over the ranges in security, and vast fields of waving grain greet the eye, where, three years ago, not a stock of artificially-produced vegetation could be seen.

> *"Where late was barrenness and waste,*
> *The perfumed blossom, bud and blade,*
> *Sweet, bashful pledges of approaching harvest,*
> *Giving cheerful promise to the hope of industry,"*

Gladden the eye, stamp contentment on happy faces, and illustrate the pleasures of industry. The farmer to his plow, the stockman to his saddle, the merchant to his ledger, the blacksmith to his forge, the carpenter to his plane, the schoolboy to his lass, and the shoemaker to his waxed-end, or *vice versa*,

The shoemaker to his	The schoolboy to his whackst
LAST	END

MICHAEL ONDAATJE

THE COLLECTED WORKS OF BILLY THE KID

Michael Ondaatje is a Canadian writer, by way of Ceylon, whose well-known works include The English Patient *and* Anil's Ghost. *An acclaimed poet as well as a novelist, he is one of many modern writers who continue to reimagine Billy the Kid.*

In this excerpt, and not without irony, not without referencing (tongue artfully in cheek) the language of those dime novelists upon which Billy the Kid's posthumous reputation was built, he muses on a world where Billy the Kid could be totally free.

THE COLLECTED WORKS OF BILLY THE KID

By Michael Ondaatje

1970

The Castle of the Spanish girl called "La Princesa" towered above the broad fertile valley . . . in the looming hills there were gold and silver mines . . . Truly, the man chosen to rule beside the loveliest woman in Mexico would be a king. The girl had chosen William H. Bonney to reign with her . . . but a massive brute named Toro Cuneo craved that honor . . .

There'd been a cattle war in Jackson County . . . He'd settled a beef with three gunquick brothers near Tucson . . . and he was weary of gunthunder and sudden death! Billy the Kid turned his cayuse south . . . splashed across the drought dried Rio Grand . . . and let the sun bake the tension out of his mind and body.

"See them sawtooth peaks, Caballo? There's a little town yonder with a real old cerveza and a fat lady who can cook Mexican food better'n anybody in the world! This lady also got a daughter . . . una muchacho . . . who's got shinin' black hair and a gleam in her brown eyes I want to see again."

And on a distant hill . . .
"He comes, be ready Soto."

"Gunshots . . . a 45 pistol! Runaway! It's a girl! She's goin' to take spill! Faster Chico!"

"AAAAAHH!"

"Hang on . . . I got yuh You're okay now Señorita."

"Gracias, Señor. You are so strong and brave . . . and very gallant!"

"Thanks, I heard shots . . . Did they scare your cayuse into runnin' away?"

"Think I can stand now, Señor . . . if you will put me down."

"Huh? Oh sorry, Señorita. I'm Billy Bonney, Señorita. I'm from up around Tucson."

"I am Marguerita Juliana de Guelva y Solanza, la Princesa de Guela."

"*La Princesa?* A real princess?"

"I am direct descendent of King Phillip of Spain. By virtue of Royal land grants, I own this land west for 200 leagues, south for 180 leagues. It is as large as some European kingdoms . . . larger than two of your American states . . . I am still a little weak. Ride with me to the castle, Señor Bonney."

"*There* Señor Bonney . . . my ancestral home. The castle and the valley farther than you can see . . . I have 20,000 cattle, almost as many horses and herds of goats, pigs, chickens. Everything my people need to live."

"WHOOOEEE! The Governor's mansion up at Phoenix would fit in one end o' that wickiup."

"Come on, Yangui! It is late . . . you must have dinner with me."

"ATTENTION! HER EXCELLENCY RETURNS!"
Thinks: "She's got a regular army!"

The man called Billy the Kid is not impressed by the magnificent richness of his surroundings. The golden cutlery means nothing . . . The priceless china and crystal matter not, and the food cooked by a French chef?—PFAAGGH!

Thinks: "I'd sooner be in Mama Rosa's kitchen eatin' tortillas an' chile with Rosita battin' them dark eyes at me!"

"This table needs a man like you, Señor Bonney. Others have occupied that chair but none so well as you."

"Gracias, Princesa . . . but I'd never feel right in it . . . if you know what I mean."

"I propose a toast, my gringo friend . . . to our meeting . . . to your gallant rescue of me!"

"I reckon I can't let a lady drink alone, Princesa."

CRASH! ! !

"He could have sunk it in my neck just as easy . . . Start talkin' hombre, 'fore I say *my* piece about that knife throwing act!"

"I am a man of action, not words, gringo! I weel crack your ribs . . . break your wrists . . . then send you back where you belong!"

"Come on, animal, I want to finish dinner!"

SOCK! !

Thinks: "If I can nail him quick I'll take the fight out of him . . . PERFECT!"

That was his Sunday punch . . . and Toro laughed at it! Now, Billy the Kid knows he's in for a struggle!

"He's got a granite jaw which means . . . I'll have to weaken him with powerful hooks to the stomach! oooowww!" THUD!

"Now it's my turn!"

"If he lays a hand on me . . . "

SWISS!

SOCK!

"I keel you gringo!"

Thinks: "My head . . . he busted my jaw!"

TOCK!

Thinks: "He's a stomper . . . "

"I keel your pet gringo Ecellencia!"

"Yuh'll take me tuh death maybe, hombre!"

"You no escape Toro now!"

"I didn't figure on escapin' Toro!"

CRACK!

"Over you go, Toro!" "Olé! Olé!"

CRASH!

"Sorry I busted the place up some, Princesa."

"You are mucho hombre, Yanqui, very much man! A man like you could help me rule this wild kingdom! Will you remain as my guest for a time?"

"I come down here to rest up some. I reckon I can do that here as well as in Mama Rosa's cantina."

(Kiss)

"That was to thank you for protecting me from Toro Cueno. I must not go on being formal with you . . . "

In the next few days, Billy the Kid was with La Princesa often. Long rides through wild country . . .

"Wait princess . . . don't get ahead of me!"

"EEEEeeii! !"

"Duck, princess!"

BANG! BANG!

"Once more Chivoto, you have saved my life, this time from that cougar. You have won my love!"

"Hold on, ma'am . . . "

Before Billy the Kid can defend himself, La Princesa Marguerita has taken him in her arms and. . . .

FILMOGRAPHY

BIG SCREEN

Billy the Kid. Vitagraph Company of America, 1911. Directed by Laurence Trimble. Tefft Johnson as Billy the Kid. Edward J. Montagne (scenario).

The Caballero's Way. Universal, 1914. Directed by Webster Cullinson. William R. Dunn as Cisco Kid. O. Henry (short story "The Caballero's Way"). The Cisco Kid was based on Billy the Kid.

The Border Terror. Universal, 1919. Directed by Harry Harvey. Vester Pegg (probably) as Cisco Kid. O. Henry (story "The Caballero's Way"). H. Tipton Steck (scenario).

In Old Arizona. Twentieth Century–Fox, 1928. Directed by Irving Cummings. Warner Baxter as Cisco Kid. O. Henry (story "The Caballero's Way"). Tom Barry and Paul Girard Smith (screenplay).

Billy the Kid. MGM, 1930. Directed by King Vidor. Johnny Mack Brown as Billy the Kid. Walter Noble Burns (book *The Saga of Billy the Kid*). Wanda Tuchock (continuity). Laurence Stallings and Charles MacArthur (dialogue).

Billy the Kid Returns. Republic Pictures, 1938. Directed by Joseph Kane. Roy Rogers as Billy the Kid. Jack Natteford (writer).

Billy the Kid Outlawed. Producers Releasing Corporation, 1940. Directed by Peter Stewart. Bob Steele as Billy the Kid. Oliver Drake (writer).

Billy the Kid in Texas. Producers Releasing Corporation, 1940. Directed by Peter Stewart. Bob Steele as Billy the Kid. Joseph O'Donnell (original screenplay).

Billy the Kid's Gun Justice. Producers Releasing Corporation, 1940. Directed by Peter Stewart. Bob Steele as Billy the Kid. Joseph O'Donnell (writer).

Billy the Kid's Range War. Producers Releasing Corporation, 1941. Directed by Peter Stewart. Bob Steele as Billy the Kid. William Lively (original screenplay).

Billy the Kid's Fighting Pals. Producers Releasing Corporation, 1941. Directed by Sam Newfield (as Sherman Scott). Bob Steele as Billy the Kid. George H. Plympton (story).

Billy the Kid. Loew's, 1941. Directed by David Miller. Robert Taylor as Billy the Kid. Walter Noble Burns (book **The Saga of Billy the Kid**). Howard Emmett Rogers and Bradbury Foote (story). Gene Fowler (screenplay).

Billy the Kid in Santa Fe. Producers Releasing Corporation, 1941. Directed by Sam Newfield (as Sherman Scott). Bob Steele as Billy the Kid. Joseph O'Donnell (story).

Billy the Kid Wanted. Producers Releasing Corporation, 1941. Directed by Sam Newfield (as Sherman Scott). Buster Crabbe as Billy the Kid. Fred Myton (original screenplay).

Billy the Kid's Round-Up. Producers Releasing Corporation, 1941. Directed by Sam Newfield (as Sherman Scott). Buster Crabbe as Billy the Kid. Fred Myton (original screenplay).

Billy the Kid Trapped. Producers Releasing Corporation, 1942. Directed by Sherman Scott. Buster Crabbe as Billy the Kid. Joseph O'Donnell (original screenplay).

Billy the Kid's Smoking Guns. Producers Releasing Corporation, 1942. Directed by Sam Newfield (as Sherman Scott). Buster Crabbe as Billy the Kid. Milton Raison and George Wallace Sayer (original screenplay).

Law and Order. Producers Releasing Corporation, 1942. Directed by Sam Newfield (as Sherman Scott). Buster Crabbe as Billy the Kid. Sam Robbins (original story and screenplay).

Sheriff of Sage Valley. Producers Releasing Corporation, 1942. Directed by Sam Newfield (as Sherman Scott). Buster Crabbe as Billy the Kid. Written by Milton Raison and George Wallace Sayer (original screenplay).

West of Tombstone. Columbia Pictures, 1942. Directed by Howard Bretherton. Gordan Demain as Billy the Kid. Maurice Geraghty (writer).

The Mysterious Rider. Producers Releasing Corporation, 1942. Directed by Sherman Scott. Buster Crabbe as Billy the Kid. Sam Robbins (original screenplay).

The Kid Rides Again. Producers Releasing Corporation, 1943. Directed by Sherman Scott. Buster Crabbe as Billy the Kid. Fred Myton (story and screenplay).

The Outlaw. Howard Hughes Productions, 1943. Directed by Howard Hughes. Jack Beutel as Billy the Kid. Jules Furthman (screenplay). Howard Hawks and Ben Hecht (writing, although uncredited).

Fugitive of the Plains. Producers Releasing Corporation, 1943. Directed by Sam Newfield. Buster Crabbe as Billy the Kid. George Wallace Sayer (original screenplay).

Western Cyclone. Producers Releasing Corporation, 1943. Directed by Sam Newfield. Buster Crabbe as Billy the Kid. Patricia Harper (original screenplay).

The Renegade. Producers Releasing Corporation, 1943. Directed by Sam Newfield. Buster Crabbe as Billy the Kid. Milton Raison and George Wallace Sayer (as George Milton) (story and screenplay).

Cattle Stampede. Producers Releasing Corporation, 1943. Directed by Sam Newfield. Buster Crabbe as Billy the Kid. Joseph O'Donnell (story and screenplay).

Blazing Frontier. Producers Releasing Company, 1943. Directed by Sam Newfield. Buster Crabbe as Billy the Kid. Patricia Harper (story and screenplay).

Four Faces West. Enterprise Productions, 1948. Directed by Alfred E. Green. Starring Joel McCrea as Ross McEwen/Billy the Kid. Eugene Manlove Rhodes (novel Paso Por Aqui). William Brent and Milarde Brent (adaptation). C. Graham Baker and Teddi Sherman (writers). Charles Bickford as Pat Garrett. William Conrad as Sheriff Egan.

Son of Billy the Kid. Western Adventures Productions Inc., 1949. Directed by Ray Taylor. William Perrott as Billy the Kid. Ron Ormond and Ira Webb (original screenplay). Lash LaRue as Marshal Jack Garrett.

The Kid from Texas. Universal, 1950. Directed by Kurt Neulmann. Audie Murphy as Billy the Kid. Robert Hardy Andrews (story and screenplay). Karl Kamb (screenplay).

I Shot Billy the Kid. William Berke Productions, 1950. Directed by William Berke. Don Barry as Billy the Kid. Orville H. Hampton (original screenplay).

Captive of Billy the Kid. Republic Pictures, 1952. Directed by Fred C. Bannon. Billy the Kid is only mentioned. M. Coates Webster and Richard Wormser (story and screenplay). Cast included Clayton Moore.

The Law vs. Billy the Kid. Columbia Pictures, 1954. Directed by William Castle. Scott Brady as Billy the Kid. Janet and Philip Stevenson (play). John T. Williams (screen story and screenplay).

The Boy from Oklahoma. Warner Bros., 1954. Directed by Michael Curtiz. Starring Tyler MacDuff as Billy the Kid. Michael Fessier (story "The Sheriff Was Scared"). Frank Davis and Winston Miller (screenplay).

Strange Lady in Town. Warner Bros., 1955. Directed by Mervyn LeRoy. Nick Adams as Billy the Kid. Frank Butler (writer), Cast included Greer Garson and Dana Andrews.

Last of the Desperadoes. Associated Film Releasing Corporation, 1955. Directed by Sam Newfield. (The Kid is mentioned, but the film centers on Pat Garrett.) Orville H. Hampton (writer).

The Parson and The Outlaw. Charles "Buddy" Rogers Productions, 1957. Directed by Oliver Drake. Anthony Dexter as Billy the Kid. Oliver Drake and John Mantley (story and screenplay).

Badman's Country. Robert E. Kent Productions, 1958. Directed by Fred F. Sears. (The Kid is only mentioned.) Orville H. Hampton (writer) / Buster Crabbe as Wyatt Earp.

The Left-Handed Gun. Haroll Productions, 1958. Directed by Arthur Penn. Paul Newman as Billy the Kid. Gore Vidal (play). Leslie Stevens (screenplay).

One-Eye Jacks. Pennebaker Productions, 1961). Directed by and starring Marlon Brando (his character is based on the Kid). Charles Neider (novel *The Authentic Death of Hendry Jones*). Guy Trosper and Clader Willingham (screenplay).

The Outlaws Is Coming. Columbia Pictures, 1965. Directed by Norman Maurer. Johnny Ginger as Billy the Kid. Norman Maurer (story). Elwood Ullman (screenplay).

Billy the Kid versus Dracula. Circle Productions Inc., 1966. Directed by William Beaudine. Chuck Courtney as Billy the Kid. Carl K. Hittleman (writer).

Chisum. Batjac Productions, 1970. Directed by Andrew V. McLaglen. Geoffrey Deuel as Billy the Kid. Andrew J. Fenady (story "Chisum and the Lincoln County Cattle War" and screenplay).

Dirty Little Billy. WRG/Dragoti Productions Ltd., 1972. Directed by Stan Dragoti. Michael J. Pollard as Billy the Kid. Charles Moss and Stan Dragoti (story and screenplay).

Pat Garrett and Billy the Kid. MGM, 1973. Directed by Sam Peckinpah. Kris Kristofferson as Billy the Kid. Rudy Wurlitzer (screenplay).

Young Guns. Morgan Creek Productions, 1988. Directed by Christopher Caine. Emilio Estevez as Billy the Kid. John Fusco (story and screenplay).

Bill and Ted's Excellent Adventure. De Laurentiis Entertainment Group, 1989. Directed by Stephen Herek. Dan Shor as Billy the Kid. Chris Matheson and Ed Solomon (story and screenplay).

Young Guns II. Morgan Creek Productions, 1990. Directed by Geoff Murphy. Emilio Estevez as Billy the Kid. John Fusco (story and screenplay).

Requiem for Billy the Kid. Cargo Films, 2006. Directed by Anne Feinsilber. Kris Kristofferson as voice of Billy the Kid. Jean-Christophe Cavallin and Anne Feinsilber (writers).

TELEVISION

The Death of Billy the Kid. Philco Television Playhouse, 1955. Directed by Gore Vidal. Paul Newman as Billy the Kid. Gore Vidal (writer).

Go West, Young Girl. Bennett/Katleman Productions, 1978. Directed by Alan J. Levi. Richard Jaeckel as Billy. George Yanok (writer).

Billy the Kid. Von Zerneck Sertner Films, 1989. Directed by William A. Graham. Val Kilmer as Billy the Kid. Gore Vidal (writer).

Purgatory. Rosemont Productions, 1999. Directed by Ulrich Edel. Donnie Wahlberg as Billy the Kid. Gordon T. Dawson (writer). Sam Shepard, Randy Quaid, and Eric Roberts also star.

Aside from movies, Billy the Kid was also portrayed in many television show series such as *Tall Man, Colt .45,* and *Maverick.*

CISCO KID
The following are films based on the character "the Cisco Kid" but otherwise not directly related to O. Henry's Cisco Kid.

The Cisco Kid. Fox Film Corporation, 1931. Directed by Irving Cummings. Warner Baxter as Cisco Kid. Alfred A. Cohn (writer).
The Return of the Cisco Kid. Twentieth Century–Fox, 1939. Directed by Herbert I. Leeds. Warner Baxter as Cisco Kid. Milton Sperling (writer).
The Cisco Kid and the Lady. Twentieth Century–Fox, 1939. Directed by Herbert I. Leeds. Cesar Romero as Cisco Kid. Stanley Rauh (story). Frances Hyland (screenplay).
Viva Cisco Kid. Twentieth Century–Fox, 1940. Directed by Norman Foster. Cesar Romero as Cisco Kid. Samuel G. Engel and Hal Long (screenplay).
The Gay Caballero. Twentieth Century–Fox, 1940. Directed by Otto Brower. Cesar Romero as Cisco Kid. Walter Bullock (story). Albert Duffy (story and screenplay). John Larkin (writer).
Lucky Cisco Kid. Twentieth Century–Fox, 1940. Directed by H. Bruce Humberstone. Cesar Romero as Cisco Kid. Julian Johnson (story). Robert Ellis (writer). Helen Logan (writer).

Ride On, Vaquero. Twentieth Century–Fox, 1941. Directed by Herbert I. Leeds. Cesar Romero as Cisco Kid. Samuel G. Engel (screenplay).

Romance of the Rio Grande. Twentieth Century–Fox, 1941. Directed by Herbert I. Leeds. Cesar Romero as Cisco Kid. Katherine Fullerton Gerould (novel Conquistador). Harold Buchman (screenplay). Samuel G. Engel (screenplay).

The Cisco Kid in Old New Mexico. Monogram Pictures, 1945. Directed by Phil Rosen. Duncan Renaldo as Cisco Kid. Betty Burbridge (original screenplay).

The Cisco Kid Returns. Monogram Pictures, 1945. Directed by John P. McCarthy. Duncan Renaldo as Cisco Kid. Betty Burbridge (original screenplay).

South of the Rio Grande. Monogram Pictures, 1945. Directed by Lambert Hillyer. Duncan Renaldo as Cisco Kid. Johnston McCulley (story). Victor Hammond and Ralph Gilbert Bettison (writers).

The Gay Cavalier. Monogram Pictures, 1946. Directed by William Nigh. Gilbert Roland as Cisco Kid. Charles Belden (original story and screenplay). Sidney Sutherland (writer).

Beauty and the Bandit. Monogram Pictures, 1946. Directed by William Nigh. Gilbert Roland as Cisco Kid. Charles Belden (original screenplay).

South of Monterey. Monogram Pictures, 1946. Directed by William Nigh. Gilbert Roland as Cisco Kid. Charles Belden (writer).

King of the Bandits. Monogram Pictures, 1947. Directed by Christy Cabanne. Duncan Renaldo as Cisco Kid. Christy Cabanne (story). Bennett Cohen (screenplay). Gilbert Roland (additional dialogue).

Riding the California Trail. Monogram Pictures, 1947. Directed by William Nigh. Gilbert Roland as Cisco Kid. Clarence Upson Young (screenplay).

Robin Hood of Monterey. Monogram Pictures, 1947. Directed by Christy Cabanne. Gilbert Roland as Cisco Kid. Bennett Cohen (original story and screenplay).

Valiant Hombre. United Artists, 1948. Directed by Wallace Fox. Duncan Renaldo as Cisco Kid. Adele S. Buffington (original screenplay).

The Gay Amigo. United Artists, 1949. Directed by Wallace Fox. Duncan Renaldo as Cisco Kid. Doris Schroeder (original screenplay).

Satan's Cradle. United Artists, 1949. Directed by Ford Beebe. Duncan Renaldo as Cisco Kid. J. Benton Chaney (original screenplay).

The Daring Caballero. United Artists, 1949. Directed by Wallace Fox. Duncan Renaldo as Cisco Kid. Frances Kavanaugh (story). Betty Burbridge (screenplay).

The Girl from San Lorenzo. United Artists, 1950. Directed by Derwin Abrahams. Duncan Renaldo as Cisco Kid. Ford Beebe (writer).

PERMISSIONS ACKNOWLEDGMENTS

An excerpt from *Gunslinger, Book 1* by Edward Dorn, originally published by Black Sparrow Press in 1968. Used by permission of Jennifer Dorn.

The Story of the Outlaw by Emerson Hough, the chapter entitled, "The Desperado," originally published in 1907.

Folk-Say, 1930, an excerpt entitled "Apocrypha of Billy the Kid," Maurice G. Fulton, originally published by University of Oklahoma Press.

From *A Vaquero of the Brush Country: The Life and Times of John D. Young* by John D. Young and J. Frank Dobie, an excerpt from the chapter entitled "Billy the Kid Interupted," copyright 1929, 1957, 1998. Used by pernission of the University of Texas Press.

Western High Spots by Jeff C. Dykes, an excerpt from the chapter entitled, "Billy the Kid Was My Friend," copyright 1977 by Jeff C. Dykes. Used by permission of the Texas A&M Development Foundation.

The Heart of the West by O. Henry, a short story, "The Caballero's Way," originally published in 1904.

Pardner of the Wind by N. Howard (Jack) Thorp (collaboration with Neil M. Clark), an excerpt from the chapter entitled,

"Billy ("The Kid") Bonney," originally published in 1941 by The Caxton Printers. Used by permission of Caxton Press.

History of "Billy the Kid" by Charles A. Siringo, Chapter 4, entitled *"The Starting of the Bloody Lincoln County War. The Murder of Tunstall. 'Billy The Kid' Is Partially Revenged When He Kills Morton and Baker.",* originally published in 1920, copyright Charles A. Siringo.

The Real Billy the Kid by Miguel Antonio Otero Jr., an excerpt from the chapter entitled, "The Lincoln County War," originally published in 1936 by Rufus Rockwell Wilson, Inc.

This excerpt from *My Life on the Frontier: 1864–1882* by Miguel Antonio Otero appears courtesy of Sunstone Press, Box 2321, Santa Fe, NM 87503; www.sonstonepress.com.

Apache Voices: Their Stories of Survival As Told To Eve Ball edited by Sherry Robinson, an excerpt from the chapter entitled, "Billy the Kid," copyright 2000 by Sherry Robinson. Used by permission of University of New Mexico Press.

Women of Wanted Men by Kit Knight, excerpts entitled "Catherine Boujeau, The Kid's Mother: 1874," "The Reverend's Wife: 1878," "Sallie Chisum, 1878: Clear Light," "Mrs. Scott Morre, 1879," "Manuela Bowdre, Christmas Day 1880," "Paulita, 1881: Widow" and "Celsa, 1881: The Year the Stars Fell," published by Potpouri Publications Company, copyright 1994 by Kit Knight. Used by permission of Kit Knight.

ABOUT THE EDITOR

Harold Dellinger is a bookseller, small press publisher, and the author of several well-received books on Missouri historical subjects. He is a former parole officer for the city of Kansas City and has long been interested in outlaw and lawman history. His previous title for The Globe Pequot Press is *Jesse James: The Best Writings on the Notorious Outlaw and His Gang*.